THE COMPLETE WORKS OF
WILLIAM SHAKESPEARE
WITH ANNOTATIONS AND
A GENERAL INTRODUCTION
BY SIDNEY LEE

VOLUME IV

THE TAMING OF THE SHREW
WITH A SPECIAL INTRODUCTION BY ALICE MEYNELL
AND AN ORIGINAL FRONTISPIECE BY ELEANOR F. BRICKDALE

BOSTON   THE JEFFERSON PRESS   NEW YORK

CONTENTS

INTRODUCTION

THERE are two plays within plays wherein Shakespeare commits extravagance: the "Hamlet" interlude and "The Taming of the Shrew." Needless to say, the inter-relation of the four plays is different; the inner play being a brief incident in the tragedy, and the outer play a mere incident in the comedy. But the inner play is in each case removed, set further than ordinary drama from the conditions of actual life, — the life of the audience seated at this table of double entertainment. Now, it seems evident that when he thus took two conventions, erected one proscenium within another, added fiction to fiction, lapped a play with a play, and proclaimed a second make-believe, Shakespeare took full advantage of this circumstance of art. He who knew the separa-

tion of drama from life knew the added separation of a
drama within a drama from life, and gave himself a fantastic permission to exceed, and not only to exceed but
to ignore, to *glisser*, to evade, to refuse us the right to
look as deep as we may look into single, ordinary and
primary drama.   Into the comedy of " The Taming of
the Shrew " we may not look, we look *upon* it.   Nor do
we, if we are wise, ask for leave to do more.   " *N'appuyons
pas*."   If we wish to pause, let it be on the slight play
which is the first and the immediate drama, — that is, the
" Induction," the comedy of Christopher Sly.   Here is
something to linger over, here are a very few things, but
rich ones; here is something human, something richly
alive, and responsible to Nature.   Through one proscenium, through one convention, we look upon that life
once removed from reality which is drama.   The " Induction " is a very small play, but a play full of slightly
scenic nature; " The Taming of the Shrew " itself is a
long play, but a play vacant of nature.   The Elizabethan
dramatist took his ease in that inn of the stage, and took
it the more whimsically in that stage-alcove, the inner
scene whereon the Player King and the Player Queen,
Petruchio and Katharine, act their parts.   Fantastic, wilful, arbitrary, defiant, unchallengeable is " The Taming
of the Shrew."   Whatever pleasure we can take in this
comedy is manifestly to be taken at a glance.   To the
Elizabethan audience the pleasure was not small ; to us
to-day it is not great.   Such as it is, it must be taken
with gaiety, without insistence, without exaction, and in
haste.   We must certainly not be either tender or stern ;

we must not incline to the pathos of mortal things.
Not long ago an essayist found out pathos in Christopher
Sly. Having looked close and sadly, and with a modern
mind, to the tinker, he erected himself again, as it were,
turned round, and told us it was this that he had discovered, — namely, pathos. It seems an undramatic
quest and an importunate suggestion; a lapse of tact, and
under the guise of more than common imagination, an
utter defect of phantasy, — this fond curiosity and this
soft heart of the modern writer. Yet if he must be
moved; and if he must compel Shakespeare to serve him
in his emotions; and if he will not keep them for his living brothers, but must spend them on the comic drama,
why then at least let him have his way with Christopher Sly and the "Induction" only; let him stop there.
Let him not intrude upon the inner play, and find the
pathos of life in that gay interior where the light heart
of drama takes sanctuary; let him not attribute pathos
to Katharine, or study Petruchio, or make a symbol of
the Pedant.

Nevertheless, this, or nearly this, is what he has in
fact done — or rather she; for a woman, once well and
honourably known for her Shakespearean studies, and
in particular for a Concordance, did point the moral of
Katharine and Bianca, making a story of the earlier girl-
hood of each, setting forth that once before had this
shrew been tamed by a strong-handed boy, — Petruchio's
precursor; that this generous nature of woman did but
wait for love and a master; and so forth. The thing
is just worthy of mention because it may stand as a per-

fect example of the kind of attention, the kind of sympathy, the seriousness, of which " The Taming of the Shrew " ought not to be the subject. Nay, it might be worth while to pretend to take such a commentary seriously for a while, in order to show the kind writer to what she would commit herself. Granting her, then, that the heroine of a tender story, a sentimental shrew honestly in need of love and a respectable master, is appropriately to be tamed by famine, cold, ignominy, insolence, and violence, to what end are these rigours practised in the play? To what end but to make of her a hypocrite — her husband the while happy to have her so? For a woman who feigns, under menace, to see a young maid where an old man stands, or a sun where the moon shines, is no other. Katharine does this for fear of the repetition of outrage — more famine, more cold, more contempt, at the hands of the strong man : the strong man of her girlish dreams, quotha! See to what a pass an earnest view of this play will bring us. But no need to confound the sentimentalist further with the monstrous morality — the merry drama. No, these sweet ways of feeling are out of place in the audience at the playing of " The Taming of the Shrew " ; and as the audience, so must the readers be. The comedy is drama, and only by concomitance and only insomuch as all composed language is literary, is it literature. And yet literature stands between it and life — nearer than life. Therefore neither to Katharine's past nor to her future have we to look, neither to her spirit nor to anything that can be called a woman's womanhood are we led by Shakespeare. She is not a woman of this world, she is a shrew of the inner stage. Let us look on her drama, not into it, and not through it. And in fact Shakespeare may have taken the convention of his comedy all the more easily because the Katharine played before him was not a woman. The squeaking Katharine who " boy'd her greatness " surely helped him to his irresponsibility. He had before him a romping youth, not a raging woman. In so far as this Katharine was a woman she was a grotesque and intolerable creature, to be overcome and broken by grotesque and intolerable means. This doubtless was the shrew of that society. She has vanished from ours. A shrew may scold, in our day, in the alleys of a town, but not in " Petruchio's house in the country "; not in the person of a beautiful, young, and well-taught woman. In Goldoni's comedies, of a century and a half later than Shakespeare's, there are still shrews. For a defect of dress, for a dowry, for a dispute with a mother-in-law, *rabbia* is the name of the lesser and earlier stages of a woman's anger, and *tutte le furie* of the greater and later. The men of those Venetian households, occupied with the choice of *paste* for the soup, and going in and out in the course of a long day on little affairs and bargainings, have for their principal preoccupation this tendency to *rabbia* and *tutte le furie* amongst the women — the ladies; let us give them the name that both Shakespeare and Goldoni give. It is to be noted that the Goldoni husband has no hope or expectation of a remedy; like Petruchio, he has no thought of appealing to the reason or the conscience of the woman; unlike Petruchio, he has no mind to quell her by force. Like Petruchio, again, he does her not so much honour as lies in a reproach; to responsible humanity belong reproof, rebuke, remonstrance, or even dislike, even forgiveness, but not to a woman married into a family of Venice. The husband in Goldoni's comedies neither hates nor pardons the furies — he does no more than evade them. If the noise will but spend itself and the daughter-in-law and the mother-in-law return to their own apartments, pacified by promises, all is well for the time. The master-mind was never more tolerant or unmoved than in this master of a tempestuous household. He makes no comment, and generalises not at all. *Il ne fait que constater.* Sufficient for the day is the storm. After a reading of Goldoni, it might be worth while — for the love of Shakespeare, but hardly for the love of this play of his — to disentangle what is Italian from what is English. We have plenty of evidence of the currency of a popular play, "Taming of a Shrew," in England in the time of Shakespeare. Other parts of Shakespeare's play are derived remotely from the Italian of Ariosto, and, moreover, the author of the comedy of which Petruchio is hero had a small piece of Italian knowledge of which the author of the tragedy that has Hamlet for hero was ignorant, — the gender, that is, of the Italian name Battista, or, as the English plays have it, Baptista. Its final vowel gave it a feminine sound, and it is a woman's name in "Hamlet," but a man's, as it should be, in "The Taming of the Shrew." This dis-

parity has of course been remarked by those who have
not thought the play last named to be the work of
Shakespeare ; but the incident is too slight to bear any
such significance. Obviously, Shakespeare might forget
his scholarship on the point of Italian Christian names,
if, as seems to be the case, we must not suppose that
he corrected it, because " Hamlet " was the later work.
Whatever may be the conflict of expert opinion as to the
entire authorship, on the external ground, the testimony
of the play itself is surely that, although Shakespeare the
manager borrowed his plot, the scenes are the writing
of Shakespeare the dramatist. " The Taming of the
Shrew " is authentically Shakespeare's to the reader.
Circumstantial evidence apart, the Shakespearean who
is in every man and woman of letters, English and
American, will not hesitate to pronounce it veritably
Shakespeare's, almost Shakespeare's worst (the " Induction " apart), but as certainly his as " Lear " itself ; yet will
be willing to accept any well-accredited origin for the
dramatic story — Italian lendings, or popular current
English horse-play, or any other. The note of the time
is no more manifest than the tone of the man of the time.
Shakespeare's tone, even when it is hardly significant
enough to be called Shakespeare's style, is assuredly to
be recognised like a voice. The note is Elizabethan ;
and the dramatists, the lyrists, the sonneteers sing it
alike ; but who would doubt the tone of the driest coup-
let in one of Shakespeare's sonnets ? Hardly more can
one doubt whose voice in literature it is that speaks a
slight speech for Bianca or for Tranio. Tranio, by the

way, is very Italian. That manner of man, who sur-
vived so buoyantly in the comedy of Molière, is evi-
dently the Arlecchino, or Harlequin, of the primitive
stage of Italy : the tricksy and shifty spirit, the trusty
rogue, the wonder-worker, the man in disguise, the Mer-
curial one. He is many times modified, and is exquis-
itely altered by the loss of his customary good luck, in
Shakespeare's " Romeo and Juliet." For when Mercutio
falls, there falls with him the gay but inhuman figure —
falls, for English literature, perhaps finally. It lives, it
takes a mortal wound at Tybalt's sword-point, it bleeds
and dies. The primitive Italian tradition is, moreover,
touched in another place, where Lucentio speaks to the
smooth Bianca of her father, behind his back, as " the old
Pantaloon." Baptista is very little of a Pantaleone; except
insomuch as he suffers deception, he is a person of sufficient dignity. And that he is subject to this deception
is a token both of the Italian and of the Shakespearean humour. Of the two—the typical Italian primitive and the single Shakespeare — it may be suspected
that it was Shakespeare who best loved a mystification ;
the word is not a good one in English, but we may quote
it from the French. to describe precisely the kind of jest.
That Shakespeare took some Puckish pleasure in that
jest we know. " The Comedy of Errors " bears witness
to this, so does " Twelfth Night," so does " All 's Well
that Ends Well." Nay., a brief mystification comes to
pass in the course of a tragedy ; it hampers the urgency
of some passage of passionate feeling ; the moment,
stretched with apprehension and dismay, is made to

include a misunderstanding, such as that of Juliet and her nurse after the death of Tybalt. What Shakespeare manifestly loved was the error, but he loved it best in the form of mystification. The beguiling of Baptista by his daughter Bianca, the denying of Vincentio by his men, and the presentation of the Pedant in his place are perfect examples of that unjust pleasantry the sufferer whereof has no defence, for no wit nor wisdom nor wariness could avail him — he is entirely in the hands of a tormentor who has all the knowledge and all the advantage, and uses them for sport with delight, and without sparing, against the aged, the reverend, or the noble. It is true that the hero — son and lover — does not follow the jest to the utmost; that is left for Arlecchino, the merry rogue without a conscience. Whoever was Shakespeare's coadjutor — if he had one, and in some scenes in the part of Bianca it seems probable—Shakespeare in person took a sharp interest in this "coney-catching." To the greater number of modern spirits it is of so little interest, and so little to be loved, as to stand somewhat between them and their dramatist, — a difference involving the very substructure of humour. There is nothing for it but a reconciliation in the most humorous "Induction." And what is this but a mystification also? Although it is not perhaps the delusion of the tinker that so takes us, but his nature under all fortunes. We have Christopher Sly in common with Shakespeare, let his lord use him as he may. Careless Shakespeare, having carried his inner play to a jolly end, with a preposterous grave moral, sweeps the persons off their little sanctuary stage, and forgets to close up the outer comedy at all ; so that we know no more of the tinker, nor of his restoration to the ale-house on the heath and to his quarrel with the ale-wife. Or the conclusion is lost. But, as it stands, the inner play carries off the victory, and the "Induction" is forgotten. The tinker ceases in the illusion of the lord's house. He ceases and vanishes, and the dramatist does not stay to have the laugh finally against him. No one waits to see Christopher Sly himself again, or to hear him attempt an indignant Marian Hacket with the re- cital of his adventure. So that the last we hear from him is the restless sigh offered by the clown to the fancy of drama and mirth : "Comes there any more of it ? . . . 'T is a very excellent piece of work, madam lady ; would 't were done."

A scientific inquiry into the evidence touching the authorship of the play in all its parts is not within the province of this short essay. But it does belong to the appreciation of the comedy, and it is in the compe- tence of a student of verse, to dwell for a moment upon the metrical testimony to the identity of the author of "Love's Labour 's Lost" and the author of "The Taming of the Shrew." Anapæsts (I speak of course of anapæsts as one may adapt the word to the use of English prosody) are rare in English literature before the eighteenth cen- tury made them its lighter favourites, and peculiarly its own, the expression of its dapper and commonplace gaiety and frolic, whether in the age of Anne or when Mrs. Thrale was rendering epigrams from the French. The sixteenth and seventeenth centuries meddled little with this kind of verse. The iambic movement, the noble gait of English poetry, rarely interrupted by a brief shifting to the springing foot of the trochee, is, in all its composure and simplicity, the very pace of these two great centuries. Lyrical poetry goes by in procession, from the stanza of Surrey to the ode of Dryden, to that measure. The dramatist in this matter keeps step and time with the lyrist; the numbers are different, the foot is the same. And Shakespeare's rhymes in the plays are, habitually, iambic — heroic couplets. In "Love's Labour's Lost," however, occurs, among the varied short iambic rhymed verses, the altered rhythm of a rough and imperfect anapæstic verse : —

> "My lips are no common, though several they be."
> "Belonging to whom?" "To my fortunes and me."

And in "The Taming of the Shrew" is this, with — in various places — two or three more couplets like it : —

> "T was I won the wager, though you hit the white;
> And being the winner, God give you good night."

Nothing sounds stranger than such a movement in Shakespeare's verse, but the strangeness is common — with a quite evident identity of lax and careless rhythm — to the two plays.

After all, the value of this comedy is in the "Induction," and the value of the "Induction" is not only in its excellent humour, but in the external incidents — the direct allusion made here by Shakespeare to the daily landscape, the house, the householder of the Warwickshire village known to him. Only in "The Merry Wives of Windsor" and in the "Second Part of Henry IV" do we come thus near to the roads that Shakespeare walked, the heath he looked upon, the man and woman he watched brawling. "The Taming of the Shrew," if it be of earlier date than the two plays just named, has the first passages of this homely external intimacy, and Kit Sly brings us and the Past acquainted. We let the Shrew go by — the excuse for her story is that it passes; but not so the Tinker.

ALICE MEYNELL.

DRAMATIS PERSONÆ [1]

A Lord.
CHRISTOPHER SLY, a tinker.　　　　　　　　　} Persons in the
Hostess, Page, Players, Huntsmen, and Servants. } Induction.
BAPTISTA, a rich gentleman of Padua.
VINCENTIO, an old gentleman of Pisa.
LUCENTIO, son to Vincentio, in love with Bianca.
PETRUCHIO, a gentleman of Verona, a suitor to Katharina.
GREMIO,   }
HORTENSIO, } suitors to Bianca.
TRANIO,   }
BIONDELLO, } servants to Lucentio.
GRUMIO,   }
CURTIS,   } servants to Petruchio.
A Pedant.
KATHARINA, the shrew, }
BIANCA,   } daughters to Baptista.
Widow.

Tailor, Haberdasher, and Servants attending on Baptista and
Petruchio.

SCENE — *Padua, and Petruchio's country house*

[1] DRAMATIS PERSONÆ] This play was printed for the first time in the
First Folio of 1623. The piece called *The Taming of A Shrew*, on which
Shakespeare founded his work, was first published anonymously in
1594, and was reissued in 1596 and 1607. In the First Folio version of
Shakespeare's play no list of "dramatis personæ" appears, and the only
divisions noted are the following : "Actus primus, Scæna Prima," which
stands at the head of the "Induction"; "Actus Tertia"; "Actus
Quartus, Scena Prima"; and "Actus Quintus." Rowe, in his edition
of 1709, first gave a preliminary list of characters. The accepted
distribution into Acts and Scenes is due to Steevens.

INDUCTION — SCENE I

BEFORE AN ALEHOUSE ON A HEATH

Enter Hostess *and* SLY

SLY

'LL PHEEZE YOU, IN faith.

Host. A pair of stocks, you rogue!

SLY. Y' are a baggage: the Slys are no rogues; look in the chronicles; we came in with Richard Conqueror. Therefore paucas pallabris; let the world slide: sessa!

Host. You will not pay for the glasses you have burst?

SLY. No, not a denier. Go by, Jeronimy: go to thy cold bed, and warm thee.

Host. I know my remedy; I must go fetch the thirdborough. [*Exit.* 10

---

5 *paucas pallabris . . . sessa !*] "Paucas pallabris" is a corruption of the Spanish expression "pocas palabras," few words. It appears

SLY. Third, or fourth, or fifth borough, I'll answer him by law: I'll not budge an inch, boy: let him come, and kindly.   [*Falls asleep.*

Horns winded.   Enter a Lord *from hunting, with his train*

LORD. Huntsman, I charge thee, tender well my
          hounds:
Brach Merriman, the poor cur is emboss'd;

---

again in *Much Ado*, III, v, 15, in the abbreviated form " palabras."
" Let the world slide " or " Let the world slip " (Induction, ii,
140, *infra*) is a common phrase for " take things easy." Cf.
Beaumont and Fletcher's *Wit without Money*, V, 2: " Will you go
drink and *let the world slide* ? "   " Sessa ! " reappears twice in *Lear*,
III, iv, 99, and III, vi, 73 ; it seems a corruption of the Spanish
" cessa," cease, give over, be quiet.

7 *Go by, Jeronimy*] The First Folio reads, go by S. *Ieronimie*. The
ejaculation was a vulgar catchword drawn from the popular play
by Thomas Kyd, *The Spanish Tragedie . . . With the pittiful death
of old Hieronimo* (1594), III, xii, 31 : " Hieronimo beware ; go
by, go by." The phrase constantly figures in Elizabethan drama,
and implies impatience with anything disagreeable.

8 *go . . . warm thee*] Another vulgar ejaculation ; it is repeated in
Lear, III, iv, 47. The catch-phrase, which was very popular, was
possibly suggested by another scene of Kyd's *Spanish Tragedie*, II,
v, 1–12, where Hieronimo enters " in his shirt," and remarks,
" What outcries pluck me from my naked bed And chill my
throbbing heart with trembling fear ? "

9 *thirdborough*] This is Theobald's emendation (rendered necessary by
Sly's retort) of the Folio reading, *Headborough*. Both words
mean " constable."   " Thirdborough " appears as " Tharborough "
in *L. L. L.*, I, i, 185.

12–13 *let . . . kindly*] let him come, and welcome.

And couple Clowder with the deep-mouth'd brach.
Saw'st thou not, boy, how Silver made it good
At the hedge-corner, in the coldest fault?
I would not lose the dog for twenty pound.
  FIRST HUN. Why, Belman is as good as he, my lord; 20
He cried upon it at the merest loss,
And twice to-day pick'd out the dullest scent:
Trust me, I take him for the better dog.
  LORD. Thou art a fool: if Echo were as fleet,
I would esteem him worth a dozen such.
But sup them well and look unto them all:
To-morrow I intend to hunt again.
  FIRST HUN. I will, my lord.
  LORD. What's here? one dead, or drunk?   See, doth
    he breathe?
  SEC. HUN. He breathes, my lord.   Were he not
    warm'd with ale,   30
This were a bed but cold to sleep so soundly.
  LORD. O monstrous beast! how like a swine he
    lies!
Grim death, how foul and loathsome is thine image!
Sirs, I will practise on this drunken man.
What think you, if he were convey'd to bed,
Wrapp'd in sweet clothes, rings put upon his fingers,
A most delicious banquet by his bed,

---

18 *fault*] used here, much as in geology, for a breach in the con-
  tinuity of the trail.   "The cold *fault*" in *Venus and Adonis*, 694,
  is employed in the same way.   "The coldest fault" is equivalent
  to "the dullest scent," l. 22, *infra.*

And brave attendants near him when he wakes,
Would not the beggar then forget himself?
   FIRST HUN. Believe me, lord, I think he cannot
      choose.   40
   SEC. HUN. It would seem strange unto him when he
      waked.
   LORD. Even as a flattering dream or worthless fancy.
Then take him up and manage well the jest:
Carry him gently to my fairest chamber
And hang it round with all my wanton pictures:
Balm his foul head in warm distilled waters
And burn sweet wood to make the lodging sweet:
Procure me music ready when he wakes,
To make a dulcet and a heavenly sound;
And if he chance to speak, be ready straight   50
And with a low submissive reverence
Say "What is it your honour will command?"
Let one attend him with a silver basin
Full of rose-water and bestrew'd with flowers;
Another bear the ewer, the third a diaper,
And say "Will't please your lordship cool your
      hands?"
Some one be ready with a costly suit,
And ask him what apparel he will wear;
Another tell him of his hounds and horse,
And that his lady mourns at his disease: 60
Persuade him that he hath been lunatic;
And when he says he is, say that he dreams,
For he is nothing but a mighty lord.
This do and do it kindly, gentle sirs:

[6]

It will be pastime passing excellent,
If it be husbanded with modesty.

    FIRST HUN. My lord, I warrant you we will play
            our part,
As he shall think by our true diligence
He is no less than what we say he is.

    LORD. Take him up gently and to bed with him;   70
And each one to his office when he wakes.

               [Some bear out Sly. A trumpet sounds.

Sirrah, go see what trumpet 't is that sounds:

                    [Exit Servingman.

Belike, some noble gentleman that means,
Travelling some journey, to repose him here.

        Re-enter Servingman

How now! who is it?

    SERV.   An 't please your honour, players
That offer service to your lordship.

    LORD. Bid them come near.

            Enter Players

             Now, fellows, you are welcome.

    PLAYERS. We thank your honour.

    LORD. Do you intend to stay with me to-night?

---

66 *If . . . modesty*] If it be not overdone, if it be dealt with in
    moderation.
75–76 *players . . . lordship*] Strolling companies of Elizabethan actors
    were in the habit of calling at great lords' houses and offering
    to perform in their presence. Cf. *Hamlet*, II, ii.

A PLAYER. So please your lordship to accept our
duty.   80
LORD. With all my heart. This fellow I remember,
Since once he play'd a farmer's eldest son :
'T was where you woo'd the gentlewoman so well :
I have forgot your name ; but, sure, that part
Was aptly fitted and naturally perform'd.
A PLAYER. I think 't was Soto that your honour
means.
LORD. 'T is very true : thou didst it excellent.
Well, you are come to me in happy time ;
The rather for I have some sport in hand
Wherein your cunning can assist me much.   90
There is a lord will hear you play to-night :
But I am doubtful of your modesties ;
Lest over-eyeing of his odd behaviour, —
For yet his honour never heard a play, —
You break into some merry passion
And so offend him ; for I tell you, sirs,
If you should smile he grows impatient.

---

86 *A Player*] In the First Folio, and also in the old play of *A Shrew*,
for "A Player" is substituted "Sincklo," the name of a well-
known actor of the day, who is also introduced into the old
editions of *2 Hen. IV*, V, iv, and *3 Hen. VI*, III, i, as well as
into the Induction of Marston's *Malcontent.* "Soto" is doubtless
a character in some unidentified Spanish or Italian play. The
earliest English piece in which it is found is Beaumont and
Fletcher's *Women Pleased* (1620 ?).
95 *merry passion*] burst of merriment. Cf. "The over-merry spleen,"
l. 135, *infra.*

[8]

A Player. Fear not, my lord: we can contain our-
      selves,
Were he the veriest antic in the world.
    Lord. Go, sirrah, take them to the buttery,   100
And give them friendly welcome every one:
Let them want nothing that my house affords.
                    [*Exit one with the Players.*
Sirrah, go you to Barthol'mew my page,
And see him dress'd in all suits like a lady:
That done, conduct him to the drunkard's chamber;
And call him "madam," do him obeisance.
Tell him from me, as he will win my love,
He bear himself with honourable action,
Such as he hath observed in noble ladies
Unto their lords, by them accomplished: 110
Such duty to the drunkard let him do
With soft low tongue and lowly courtesy,
And say, "What is 't your honour will command,
Wherein your lady and your humble wife
May show her duty and make known her love?"
And then with kind embracements, tempting kisses,
And with declining head into his bosom,
Bid him shed tears, as being overjoy'd
To see her noble lord restored to health,
Who for this seven years hath esteemed him   120
No better than a poor and loathsome beggar:
And if the boy have not a woman's gift
To rain a shower of commanded tears,
An onion will do well for such a shift,
Which in a napkin being close convey'd

Shall in despite enforce a watery eye.
See this dispatch'd with all the haste thou canst :
Anon I 'll give thee more instructions. [*Exit a Servingman.*
I know the boy will well usurp the grace,
Voice, gait and action of a gentlewoman : 130
I long to hear him call the drunkard husband,
And how my men will stay themselves from laughter
When they do homage to this simple peasant.
I 'll in to counsel them ; haply my presence
May well abate the over-merry spleen
Which otherwise would grow into extremes. [*Exeunt.*

SCENE II—A BEDCHAMBER IN THE LORD'S HOUSE

Enter aloft SLY, *with* Attendants ; *some with apparel, others with
basin and ewer and other appurtenances, and* Lord

SLY. For God's sake, a pot of small ale.

FIRST SERV. Will 't please your lordship drink a cup
of sack ?

SEC. SERV. Will 't please your honour taste of these
conserves ?

THIRD SERV. What raiment will your honour wear
to-day ?

SLY. I am Christophero Sly ; call not me " honour "
nor " lordship :" I ne'er drank sack in my life ; and if
you give me any conserves, give me conserves of beef :
ne'er ask me what raiment I 'll wear ; for I have no

---

135 *over-merry spleen*] Cf. note on l. 95, *supra.*

more doublets than backs, no more stockings than legs,
nor no more shoes than feet; nay, sometime more feet
than shoes, or such shoes as my toes look through the 10
overleather.

LORD. Heaven cease this idle humour in your honour!
O, that a mighty man of such descent,
Of such possessions and so high esteem,
Should be infused with so foul a spirit!

SLY. What, would you make me mad? Am not I
Christopher Sly, old Sly's son of Burton-heath, by birth
a pedlar, by education a card-maker, by transmutation a
bear-herd, and now by present profession a tinker? Ask
Marian Hacket, the fat ale-wife of Wincot, if she know 20
me not: if she say I am not fourteen pence on the score
for sheer ale, score me up for the lyingest knave in Christendom. What! I am not bestraught: here's —

THIRD SERV. O, this it is that makes your lady
      mourn!

SEC. SERV. O, this is it that makes your servants
      droop!

---

17 *Burton-heath*] The village of Barton-on-the-heath, the home of
Shakespeare's aunt, the wife of Edmund Lambert.

20 *Marian Hacket . . . Wincot*] Wincot, a small hamlet within four
miles of Stratford-on-Avon, is in the parish of Quinton. There a
family of Hackets is noticed in the parish registers. The Warwickshire poet, Sir Aston Cokain, identified Wincot, as noticed by Sly,
with Wilnecote (pronounced Wincot), a village in North Warwickshire. Others identify it with Wilmcote, the native place of
Shakespeare's mother, which is also popularly pronounced Wincot.
But Shakespeare's reference is doubtless to Wincot in Quinton
parish.

[11]

LORD. Hence comes it that your kindred shuns your
      house,
As beaten hence by your strange lunacy.
O noble lord, bethink thee of thy birth,
Call home thy ancient thoughts from banishment,
And banish hence these abject lowly dreams.   30
Look how thy servants do attend on thee,
Each in his office ready at thy beck.
Wilt thou have music? hark! Apollo plays,   [*Music.*
And twenty caged nightingales do sing:
Or wilt thou sleep? we'll have thee to a couch
Softer and sweeter than the lustful bed
On purpose trimm'd up for Semiramis.
Say thou wilt walk; we will bestrew the ground:
Or wilt thou ride? thy horses shall be trapp'd,
Their harness studded all with gold and pearl.   40
Dost thou love hawking? thou hast hawks will
      soar
Above the morning lark: or wilt thou hunt?
Thy hounds shall make the welkin answer them,
And fetch shrill echoes from the hollow earth.
    FIRST SERV. Say thou wilt course; thy greyhounds
      are as swift
As breathed stags, ay, fleeter than the roe.
    SEC. SERV. Dost thou love pictures? we will fetch
      thee straight
Adonis painted by a running brook,
And Cytherea all in sedges hid,
Which seem to move and wanton with her breath,   50
Even as the waving sedges play with wind.

LORD. We 'll show thee Io as she was a maid
And how she was beguiled and surprised,
As lively painted as the deed was done.
   THIRD SERV. Or Daphne roaming through a thorny
            wood,
Scratching her legs that one shall swear she bleeds,
And at that sight shall sad Apollo weep,
So workmanly the blood and tears are drawn.
   LORD. Thou art a lord and nothing but a lord:
Thou hast a lady far more beautiful   60
Than any woman in this waning age.
   FIRST SERV. And till the tears that she hath shed
            for thee
Like envious floods o'er-run her lovely face,
She was the fairest creature in the world ;
And yet she is inferior to none.
   SLY. Am I a lord ? and have I such a lady ?
Or do I dream ? or have I dream'd till now ?
I do not sleep : I see, I hear, I speak ;
I smell sweet savours and I feel soft things :
Upon my life, I am a lord indeed,   70
And not a tinker nor Christophero Sly.
Well, bring our lady hither to our sight ;
And once again, a pot o' the smallest ale.
   SEC. SERV. Will 't please your mightiness to wash
            your hands ?
O, how we joy to see your wit restored !
O, that once more you knew but what you are !
These fifteen years you have been in a dream ;
Or when you waked, so waked as if you slept.

[13]

SLY. These fifteen years! by my fay, a goodly nap.
But did I never speak of all that time?   80
FIRST SERV. O, yes, my lord, but very idle words:
For though you lay here in this goodly chamber,
Yet would you say ye were beaten out of door;
And rail upon the hostess of the house;
And say you would present her at the leet,
Because she brought stone jugs and no seal'd quarts:
Sometimes you would call out for Cicely Hacket.
SLY. Ay, the woman's maid of the house.
THIRD SERV. Why, sir, you know no house nor no
                such maid,
Nor no such men as you have reckon'd up,   90
As Stephen Sly and old John Naps of Greece
And Peter Turph and Henry Pimpernell
And twenty more such names and men as these
Which never were nor no man ever saw.
SLY. Now Lord be thanked for my good amends!
ALL. Amen.
SLY. I thank thee: thou shalt not lose by it.

Enter the Page *as a lady, attended*

PAGE. How fares my noble lord?
SLY. Marry, I fare well; for here is cheer enough.
Where is my wife?   100
PAGE. Here, noble lord: what is thy will with her?
SLY. Are you my wife and will not call me husband?
My men should call me "lord": I am your good-man.

---

86 *seal'd quarts*] quart pots certified by an official stamp.
91 *Greece*] Doubtless a misreading of Greet, a hamlet in Gloucester-
    shire, not far from Stratford-on-Avon.

PAGE. My husband and my lord, my lord and
     husband ;
I am your wife in all obedience.

SLY. I know it well. What must I call her ?

LORD. Madam.

SLY. Al'ce madam, or Joan madam ?

LORD. " Madam " and nothing else : so lords call
     ladies.

SLY. Madam wife, they say that I have dream'd   110
And slept above some fifteen year or more.

PAGE. Ay, and the time seems thirty unto me,
Being all this time abandon'd from your bed.

SLY. 'T is much. Servants, leave me and her alone.
Madam, undress you and come now to bed.

PAGE. Thrice-noble lord, let me entreat of you
To pardon me yet for a night or two ;
Or, if not so, until the sun be set :
For your physicians have expressly charged,
In peril to incur your former malady,   120
That I should yet absent me from your bed :
I hope this reason stands for my excuse.

SLY. Ay, it stands so that I may hardly tarry so
long. But I would be loath to fall into my dreams
again : I will therefore tarry in despite of the flesh and
the blood.

Enter a Messenger

MESS. Your honour's players, hearing your amend-
     ment,
Are come to play a pleasant comedy ;

[15]

For so your doctors hold it very meet,
Seeing too much sadness hath congeal'd your blood,
And melancholy is the nurse of frenzy :   130
Therefore they thought it good you hear a play
And frame your mind to mirth and merriment,
Which bars a thousand harms and lengthens life.

SLY. Marry, I will, let them play it. Is not a comonty
a Christmas gambold or a tumbling-trick ?

PAGE. No, my good lord ; it is more pleasing stuff.

SLY. What, household stuff ?

PAGE. It is a kind of history.

SLY. Well, we 'll see 't. Come, madam wife, sit by my
side and let the world slip : we shall ne'er be younger.   140

Flourish

---

134 *comonty*] comedy. In the old play there figures a similar blunder
" comoditie " (for " comedy ").
140 *let the world slip*] Cf. note on Induction, i, 5, *supra.*

[16]

ACT FIRST — SCENE I — PADUA

A PUBLIC PLACE

Enter LUCENTIO *and his man* TRANIO

LUCENTIO

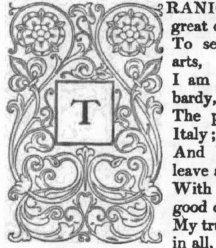

RANIO, SINCE FOR THE
great desire I had
To see fair Padua, nursery of
arts,
I am arrived for fruitful Lom-
bardy,
The pleasant garden of great
Italy;
And by my father's love and
leave am arm'd
With his good will and thy
good company,
My trusty servant, well approved
in all,
Here let us breathe and haply institute
A course of learning and ingenious studies.
Pisa renowned for grave citizens   10

---

10 *Pisa . . . citizens*] The line is repeated, IV, ii, 95, *infra.*

Gave me my being and my father first,
A merchant of great traffic through the world,
Vincentio, come of the Bentivolii.
Vincentio's son brought up in Florence
It shall become to serve all hopes conceived,
To deck his fortune with his virtuous deeds:
And therefore, Tranio, for the time I study,
Virtue and that part of philosophy
Will I apply that treats of happiness
By virtue specially to be achieved. 20

Tell me thy mind; for I have Pisa left
And am to Padua come, as he that leaves
A shallow plash to plunge him in the deep,
And with satiety seeks to quench his thirst.

TRA. *Mi perdonato*, gentle master mine,
I am in all affected as yourself;
Glad that you thus continue your resolve
To suck the sweets of sweet philosophy.
Only, good master, while we do admire
This virtue and this moral discipline, 30
Let's be no stoics nor no stocks, I pray;
Or so devote to Aristotle's checks
As Ovid be an outcast quite abjured:
Balk logic with acquaintance that you have,
And practise rhetoric in your common talk;

---

32 *checks*] rebukes, reproofs. This is the original reading, which
    modern editors needlessly change to *ethics*.
34 *Balk*] The word literally means "separate," or "discriminate."
    Hence "balk logic" is equivalent to "argue or wrangle" after
    the manner of logicians.

Music and poesy use to quicken you;
The mathematics and the metaphysics,
Fall to them as you find your stomach serves you;
No profit grows where is no pleasure ta'en:
In brief, sir, study what you most affect.   40
   Luc. Gramercies, Tranio, well dost thou advise.
If, Biondello, thou wert come ashore,
We could at once put us in readiness,
And take a lodging fit to entertain
Such friends as time in Padua shall beget.
But stay a while: what company is this?
   Tra. Master, some show to welcome us to town.

Enter Baptista, Katharina, Bianca, Gremio, *and* Hortensio.
Lucentio *and* Tranio *stand by*

   Bap. Gentlemen, importune me no farther,
For how I firmly am resolved you know;
That is, not to bestow my youngest daughter   50
Before I have a husband for the elder:
If either of you both love Katharina,
Because I know you well and love you well,
Leave shall you have to court her at your pleasure.
   Gre. [*Aside*] To cart her rather: she's too rough for me.
There, there, Hortensio, will you any wife?
   Kath. I pray you, sir, is it your will
To make a stale of me amongst these mates?

---

47 *Gremio*] In a stage-direction of the Folios this character is here sug-
   gestively described as " Gremio a Pantelowne."   Cf. III, i, 36, *infra*.
58 *stale*] commonly interpreted as "butt" or "laughing-stock."   But

HOR. Mates, maid! how mean you that? no mates
  for you,
Unless you were of gentler, milder mould.   60
 KATH. I' faith, sir, you shall never need to fear:
I wis it is not half way to her heart ;
But if it were, doubt not her care should be
To comb your noddle with a three-legg'd stool
And paint your face and use you like a fool.
 HOR. From all such devils, good Lord deliver us!
 GRE. And me too, good Lord!
 TRA. Husht, master! here's some good pastime
  toward:
That wench is stark mad or wonderful froward.
 LUC. But in the other's silence do I see   70
Maid's mild behaviour and sobriety.
Peace, Tranio!
 TRA. Well said, master; mum! and gaze your fill.
 BAP. Gentlemen, that I may soon make good
What I have said, Bianca, get you in:
And let it not displease thee, good Bianca,
For I will love thee ne'er the less, my girl.
 KATH. A pretty peat! it is best
Put finger in the eye, an she knew why.
 BIAN. Sister, content you in my discontent. 80
Sir, to your pleasure humbly I subscribe:
My books and instruments shall be my company,
On them to look and practise by myself.

---

  it is sometimes used in the sense of "common harlot." A quibble
  on "stalemate" (in chess) is suggested.
78 *peat*] archaic form of "pet," "darling."

LUC. Hark, Tranio! thou may'st hear Minerva
    speak.
HOR. Signior Baptista, will you be so strange?
Sorry am I that our good will effects
Bianca's grief.
GRE.   Why will you mew her up,
Signior Baptista, for this fiend of hell,
And make her bear the penance of her tongue?
   BAP. Gentlemen, content ye; I am resolved: 90
Go in, Bianca: [*Exit Bianca.*
And for I know she taketh most delight
In music, instruments and poetry,
Schoolmasters will I keep within my house,
Fit to instruct her youth. If you, Hortensio,
Or Signior Gremio, you, know any such,
Prefer them hither; for to cunning men
I will be very kind, and liberal
To mine own children in good bringing-up.
And so farewell. Katharina, you may stay;   100
For I have more to commune with Bianca.   [*Exit.*
   KATH. Why, and I trust I may go too, may I not?
What, shall I be appointed hours; as though, belike,
I knew not what to take, and what to leave, ha? [*Exit.*
   GRE. You may go to the devil's dam: your gifts are
so good, here's none will hold you. Their love is not so

---

85 *will . . . strange*] will you act so strangely, follow so strange a
    course?
106 *Their love*] The good will of Baptista and Bianca (towards
    us). The substitution of *Our* for the old reading *Their* seems
    unnecessary.

great, Hortensio, but we may blow our nails together,
and fast it fairly out: our cake's dough on both sides.
Farewell: yet, for the love I bear my sweet Bianca,
if I can by any means light on a fit man to teach
her that wherein she delights, I will wish him to her
father.   111

HOR. So will I, Signior Gremio: but a word, I pray.
Though the nature of our quarrel yet never brooked parle,
know now, upon advice, it toucheth us both, that we may
yet again have access to our fair mistress, and be happy
rivals in Bianca's love, to labour and effect one thing
specially.

GRE. What's that, I pray?

HOR. Marry, sir, to get a husband for her sister.

GRE. A husband! a devil.

HOR. I say, a husband.   120

GRE. I say, a devil. Thinkest thou, Hortensio,
though her father be very rich, any man is so very
a fool to be married to hell?

HOR. Tush, Gremio, though it pass your patience and
mine to endure her loud alarums, why, man, there be
good fellows in the world, an a man could light on them,
would take her with all her faults, and money enough. 127

GRE. I cannot tell; but I had as lief take her dowry

---

107 *we may blow our nails together*] we may twiddle our thumbs; we are
out of it.

108 *our cake's dough*] a common proverbial phrase meaning "it is all
up with us." The phrase is repeated, V, i, 125, *infra*.

111 *wish*] recommend. The word is twice used in the same sense,
infra, I, ii, 58, 62.

with this condition, to be whipped at the high-cross every morning.

HOR. Faith, as you say, there's small choice in rotten apples. But come; since this bar in law makes us friends, it shall be so far forth friendly maintained till by helping Baptista's eldest daughter to a husband we set his youngest free for a husband, and then have to 't afresh. Sweet Bianca! Happy man be his dole! He that runs fastest gets the ring. How say you, Signior Gremio?

GRE. I am agreed; and would I had given him the best horse in Padua to begin his wooing that would thoroughly woo her, wed her and bed her and rid the house of her! Come on. [*Exeunt Gremio and Hortensio.* 140

TRA. I pray, sir, tell me, is it possible
That love should of a sudden take such hold?

LUC. O Tranio, till I found it to be true,
I never thought it possible or likely;
But see, while idly I stood looking on,
I found the effect of love in idleness:
And now in plainness do confess to thee,
That art to me as secret and as dear
As Anna to the Queen of Carthage was,
Tranio, I burn, I pine, I perish, Tranio,   150
If I achieve not this young modest girl.

129 *high-cross*] the cross usually found set up in the market place of a town.

135 *Happy man be his dole*] A common proverbial greeting equivalent to "good luck be with him." "Dole" means "lot" or "share."

136 *the ring*] the prize in a running match; a proverbial phrase.

[23]

Counsel me, Tranio, for I know thou canst ;
Assist me, Tranio, for I know thou wilt.

TRA. Master, it is no time to chide you now ;
Affection is not rated from the heart :
If love have touch'd you, nought remains but so,
" Redime te captum quam queas minimo."

LUC. Gramercies, lad, go forward ; this contents :
The rest will comfort, for thy counsel 's sound.

TRA. Master, you look'd so longly on the maid,   160
Perhaps you mark'd not what 's the pith of all.

LUC. O yes, I saw sweet beauty in her face,
Such as the daughter of Agenor had,
That made great Jove to humble him to her hand,
When with his knees he kiss'd the Cretan strond.

TRA. Saw you no more ? mark'd you not how her sister
Began to scold and raise up such a storm
That mortal ears might hardly endure the din ?

LUC. Tranio, I saw her coral lips to move
And with her breath she did perfume the air :   170
Sacred and sweet was all I saw in her.

TRA. Nay, then, 't is time to stir him from his trance.
I pray, awake, sir : if you love the maid,
Bend thoughts and wits to achieve her.   Thus it stands :
Her elder sister is so curst and shrewd

---

155 *rated*] scolded, driven out by chiding.
157 "*Redime* . . . *minimo*"] " Yield thyself captive with the least possible resistance " ; a misquotation, from Lily's grammar, of a line in Terence, *Eunuch.*, I, i, 29, 30 : " Quid agas, nisi ut te *redimas captum quam queas minimo.*"
163 *daughter of Agenor*] Europa.

[24]

That till the father rid his hands of her,
Master, your love must live a maid at home;
And therefore has he closely mew'd her up,
Because she will not be annoy'd with suitors.

Luc. Ah, Tranio, what a cruel father's he!   180
But art thou not advised, he took some care
To get her cunning schoolmasters to instruct her?

Tra. Ay, marry, am I, sir; and now 't is plotted.

Luc. I have it, Tranio.

Tra.   Master, for my hand,
Both our inventions meet and jump in one.

Luc. Tell me thine first.

Tra.   You will be schoolmaster
And undertake the teaching of the maid:
That 's your device.

Luc.   It is: may it be done?

Tra. Not possible; for who shall bear your part,
And be in Padua here Vincentio's son;   190
Keep house and ply his book, welcome his friends,
Visit his countrymen and banquet them?

Luc. Basta; content thee, for I have it full.
We have not yet been seen in any house,
Nor can we be distinguish'd by our faces
For man or master; then it follows thus;
Thou shalt be master, Tranio, in my stead,
Keep house and port and servants, as I should:
I will some other be; some Florentine,
Some Neapolitan, or meaner man of Pisa.   200

193 *Basta*] "Enough;" the word is both Spanish and Italian.
198 *port*] magnificence or pomp.

'T is hatch'd and shall be so : Tranio, at once
Uncase thee ; take my colour'd hat and cloak :
When Biondello comes, he waits on thee ;
But I will charm him first to keep his tongue.
   TRA. So had you need.
In brief, sir, sith it your pleasure is,
And I am tied to be obedient,
For so your father charged me at our parting ;
" Be serviceable to my son," quoth he,
Although I think 't was in another sense ;   210
I am content to be Lucentio,
Because so well I love Lucentio.
   LUC. Tranio, be so, because Lucentio loves :
And let me be a slave, to achieve that maid
Whose sudden sight hath thrall'd my wounded eye.
Here comes the rogue.

Enter BIONDELLO

                        Sirrah, where have you been ?
   BION. Where have I been ! Nay, how now ! where
are you ? Master, has my fellow Tranio stolen your
clothes ? Or you stolen his ? or both ? pray, what 's the
news ?
   LUC. Sirrah, come hither : 't is no time to jest,   220
And therefore frame your manners to the time.
Your fellow Tranio here, to save my life,
Puts my apparel and my countenance on,
And I for my escape have put on his ;
For in a quarrel since I came ashore

I kill'd a man and fear I was descried :
Wait you on him, I charge you, as becomes,
While I make way from hence to save my life :
You understand me ?

BION.   I, sir ! ne'er a whit.

LUC. And not a jot of Tranio in your mouth :   230
Tranio is changed into Lucentio.

BION. The better for him : would I were so too !

TRA. So could I, faith, boy, to have the next wish
        after,
That Lucentio indeed had Baptista's youngest daughter.
But, sirrah, not for my sake, but your master's, I advise
You use your manners discreetly in all kind of com-
        panies :
When I am alone, why, then I am Tranio ;
But in all places else your master Lucentio.   238

LUC. Tranio, let 's go : one thing more rests, that thyself execute, to make one among these wooers : if thou
ask me why, sufficeth, my reasons are both good and
weighty.   [*Exeunt.*

The presenters above speak

FIRST SERV. My lord, you nod ; you do not mind the
        play.

SLY. Yes, by Saint Anne, do I. A good matter,
surely : comes there any more of it ?

PAGE. My lord, 't is but begun.

SLY. 'T is a very excellent piece of work, madam
lady : would 't were done !   [*They sit and mark.*

[27]

SCENE II—PADUA

BEFORE HORTENSIO'S HOUSE

Enter PETRUCHIO *and his man* GRUMIO

PET. Verona, for a while I take my leave,
To see my friends in Padua, but of all
My best beloved and approved friend,
Hortensio ; and I trow this is his house.
Here, sirrah Grumio ; knock, 1 say.

GRU. Knock, sir ! whom should I knock ? is there
any man has rebused your worship ?

PET. Villain, I say, knock me here soundly.

GRU. Knock you here, sir ! why, sir, what am I, sir,
that I should knock you here, sir ?   10

PET. Villain, I say, knock me at this gate
And rap me well, or I 'll knock your knave's pate.

GRU. My master is grown quarrelsome. I should
         knock you first,
And then I know after who comes by the worst.

PET. Will it not be ?
Faith, sirrah, an you 'll not knock, I 'll ring it ;
I 'll try how you can *sol, fa,* and sing it.
                          [*He wrings him by the ears.*

GRU. Help, masters, help ! my master is mad.

PET. Now, knock when I bid you, sirrah villain !

---

8 *knock me here*] knock for me here; "me" is a redundant dative,
which was common in Elizabethan English.

Enter HORTENSIO

HOR. How now ! what's the matter ? My old friend 30
Grumio ! and my good friend Petruchio ! How do you
all at Verona ?

PET. Signior Hortensio, come you to part the fray ?
"Con tutto il core ben trovato," may I say.

HOR. " Alla nostra casa ben venuto, molto honorato
signor mio Petrucio."
Rise, Grumio, rise : we will compound this quarrel.

GRU. Nay, 't is no matter, sir, what he 'leges in Latin.
If this be not a lawful cause for me to leave his service,
look you, sir, he bid me knock him and rap him soundly, 30
sir : well, was it fit for a servant to use his master so, being perhaps, for aught I see, two-and-thirty, a pip out ?
Whom would to God I had well knock'd at first,
Then had not Grumio come by the worst.

PET. A senseless villain ! Good Hortensio,
I bade the rascal knock upon your gate
And could not get him for my heart to do it.

GRU. Knock at the gate ! O heavens ! Spake you
not these words plain, "Sirrah, knock me here, rap me
here, knock me well, and knock me soundly "? And 40
come you now with, " knocking at the gate "?

PET. Sirrah, be gone, or talk not, I advise you.

HOR. Petruchio, patience ; I am Grumio's pledge :

---

32 *two-and-thirty, a pip out*] Pip is a spot on playing cards. The allusion is to an old card game, called "bone ace," or "one and
thirty ;" see IV, ii, 57, *infra.* Cf. Massinger's *Fatal Dowry*, II, ii :
"[You] are *thirty-two* years old, which is *a pip out.*"

[29]

Why, this 's a heavy chance 'twixt him and you,
Your ancient, trusty, pleasant servant Grumio.
And tell me now, sweet friend, what happy gale
Blows you to Padua here from old Verona?
    PET. Such wind as scatters young men through the
        world,
To seek their fortunes farther than at home,
Where small experience grows.   But in a few,   50
Signior Hortensio, thus it stands with me:
Antonio, my father, is deceased;
And I have thrust myself into this maze,
Haply to wive and thrive as best I may:
Crowns in my purse I have and goods at home,
And so am come abroad to see the world.
    HOR. Petruchio, shall I then come roundly to thee,
And wish thee to a shrewd ill-favour'd wife?
Thou 'ldst thank me but a little for my counsel:
And yet I 'll promise thee she shall be rich,   60
And very rich: but thou 'rt too much my friend,
And I 'll not wish thee to her.
    PET. Signior Hortensio, 'twixt such friends as we
Few words suffice; and therefore, if thou know
One rich enough to be Petruchio's wife,
As wealth is burden of my wooing dance,
Be she as foul as was Florentius' love,

---

57 *come roundly*] speak bluntly or outspokenly. Cf. *infra*, III, ii, 210,
   "take it on you so *roundly*," and IV, iv, 102, " I 'll *roundly* go about
   her."
67 *Florentius' love*] Gower in his *Confessio Amantis* tells the old story
   of the knight Florent or Florentius, who swore to marry a

As old as Sibyl, and as curst and shrewd
As Socrates' Xanthippe, or a worse,
She moves me not, or not removes, at least,   70
Affection's edge in me, were she as rough
As are the swelling Adriatic seas :
I come to wive it wealthily in Padua ;
If wealthily, then happily in Padua.

GRU. Nay, look you, sir, he tells you flatly what his
mind is : why, give him gold enough and marry him to
a puppet or an aglet-baby ; or an old trot with ne'er a
tooth in her head, though she have as many diseases as
two and fifty horses : why, nothing comes amiss, so
money comes withal.   80

HOR. Petruchio, since we are stepp'd thus far in,
I will continue that I broach'd in jest.
I can, Petruchio, help thee to a wife
With wealth enough and young and beauteous,
Brought up as best becomes a gentlewoman :
Her only fault, and that is faults enough,
Is that she is intolerable curst
And shrewd and froward, so beyond all measure,

---

hideous hag in consideration of her giving him the answer to a
riddle, which he was pledged either to solve or to die. The "Wife
of Bath" tells the same story, though the knight is given no name,
in Chaucer's *Canterbury Tales*.

68 *As old as Sibyl*] Cf. "As old as Sibylla," *Merch. of Ven.*, I, ii, 119,
note.

79 *two and fifty horses*] The "fifty diseases of a horse" were proverbial.
Cf. *Yorkshire Tragedy* : "The fifty diseases stop thee." The
numeral in "two and fifty horses" strikes a characteristic note of
exaggeration.

[31]

That, wére my state far worser than it is,
I would not wed her for a mine of gold.   90

    PET. Hortensio, peace ! thou know'st not gold's effect :
Tell me her father's name and 't is enough ;
For I will board her, though she chide as loud
As thunder when the clouds in autumn crack.

    HOR. Her father is Baptista Minola,
An affable and courteous gentleman :
Her name is Katharina Minola,
Renown'd in Padua for her scolding tongue.

    PET. I know her father, though I know not her ;
And he knew my deceased father well.   100
I will not sleep, Hortensio, till I see her ;
And therefore let me be thus bold with you
To give you over at this first encounter,
Unless you will accompany me thither.

    GRU. I pray you, sir, let him go while the humour
lasts. O' my word, an she knew him as well as I do,
she would think scolding would do little good upon him :
she may perhaps call him half a score knaves or so : why,
that's nothing ; an he begin once, he 'll rail in his rope-
tricks. I 'll tell you what, sir, an she stand him but a
little, he will throw a figure in her face and so disfigure

102-103 *let me . . . encounter*] let me be so frank as to tell you that I
    shall abandon you at our first meeting.

109-110 *rope-tricks*] Cf. *Rom. and Jul.*, II, iv, 141-142 : " What saucy
    merchant was this that was so full of his *ropery*," *i. e.* " roguery."
    But the use of " figure (of speech) " in the next sentence suggests
    that Grumio is mispronouncing " rhetoric " when he employs the
    word " rope-tricks."

111 *figure*] a figure of speech. Perhaps there is a quibbling reference

her with it that she shall have no more eyes to see
withal than a cat. You know him not, sir.   113

  HOR. Tarry, Petruchio, I must go with thee;
For in Baptista's keep my treasure is:
He hath the jewel of my life in hold,
His youngest daughter, beautiful Bianca;
And her withholds from me and other more,
Suitors to her and rivals in my love;
Supposing it a thing impossible,   120
For those defects I have before rehearsed,
That ever Katharina will be woo'd;
Therefore this order hath Baptista ta'en,
That none shall have access unto Bianca
Till Katharine the curst have got a husband.

  GRU. Katharine the curst!
A title for a maid of all titles the worst.

  HOR. Now shall my friend Petruchio do me grace;
And offer me disguised in sober robes
To old Baptista as a schoolmaster   130
Well seen in music, to instruct Bianca;
That so I may, by this device, at least
Have leave and leisure to make love to her,
And unsuspected court her by herself.

  GRU. Here's no knavery! See, to beguile the old
folks, how the young folks lay their heads together!

---

to the common phrase about "setting the ten commandments
in your face," which meant using the ten fingers or the fists for
purposes of assault.
113 *a cat*] The cat was commonly reputed to be purblind or blear-eyed
by day, though well able to see in the dark.
  8   [33]

Enter GREMIO, *and* LUCENTIO *disguised*

Master, master, look about you : who goes there, ha ?
  HOR. Peace, Grumio ! it is the rival of my love.
Petruchio, stand by a while.
  GRU. A proper stripling and an amorous !   140
  GRE. O, very well ; I have perused the note.
Hark you, sir ; I 'll have them very fairly bound :
All books of love, see that at any hand ;
And see you read no other lectures to her :
You understand me : over and beside
Signior Baptista's liberality,
I 'll mend it with a largess. Take your paper too,
And let me have them very well perfumed :
For she is sweeter than perfume itself
To whom they go to. What will you read to her ?   150
  LUC. Whate'er I read to her, I 'll plead for you
As for my patron, stand you so assured,
As firmly as yourself were still in place :
Yea, and perhaps with more successful words
Than you, unless you were a scholar, sir.
  GRE. O this learning, what a thing it is !
  GRU. O this woodcock, what an ass it is !
  PET. Peace, sirrah !
  HOR. Grumio, mum ! God save you, Signior Gremio.

---

147 *Take your paper too*] *Paper* is the old reading, for which Pope
and most succeeding editors substitute *papers*. The reference seems to be to the "note" or list of books, mentioned in
line 141. "Them," in line 148, doubtless refers to the books
themselves.

GRE. And you are well met, Signior Hortensio.   160
Trow you whither I am going? To Baptista Minola.
I promised to inquire carefully
About a schoolmaster for the fair Bianca:
And by good fortune I have lighted well
On this young man, for learning and behaviour
Fit for her turn, well read'in poetry
And other books, good ones, I warrant ye.

   HOR. 'T is well; and I have met a gentleman
Hath promised me to help me to another,
A fine musician to instruct our mistress;   170
So shall I no whit be behind in duty
To fair Bianca, so beloved of me.

   GRE. Beloved of me; and that my deeds shall prove.

   GRU. And that his bags shall prove.

   HOR. Gremio, 't is now no time to vent our love:
Listen to me, and if you speak me fair,
I 'll tell you news indifferent good for either.
Here is a gentleman whom by chance I met,
Upon agreement from us to his liking,
Will undertake to woo curst Katharine,   180
Yea, and to marry her, if her dowry please.

   GRE. So said, so done, is well.
Hortensio, have you told him all her faults?

   PET. I know she is an irksome brawling scold:
If that be all, masters, I hear no harm.

   GRE. No, say'st me so, friend? What countryman?

   PET. Born in Verona, old Antonio's son:
My father dead, my fortune lives for me;
And I do hope good days and long to see.

GRE. O sir, such a life, with such a wife, were
    strange !   190
But if you have a stomach, to 't i' God's name :
You shall have me assisting you in all.
But will you woo this wild-cat?
    PET.   Will I live?
    GRU. Will he woo her? ay, or I 'll hang her.
    PET. Why came I hither but to that intent?
Think you a little din can daunt mine ears?
Have I not in my time heard lions roar?
Have I not heard the sea puff'd up with winds
Rage like an angry boar chafed with sweat?
Have I not heard great ordnance in the field,   200
And heaven's artillery thunder in the skies?
Have I not in a pitched battle heard
Loud 'larums, neighing steeds, and trumpets' clang?
And do you tell me of a woman's tongue,
That gives not half so great a blow to hear
As will a chestnut in a farmer's fire?
Tush, tush ! fear boys with bugs.
    GRU.   For he fears none.
    GRE. Hortensio, hark :
This gentleman is happily arrived,
My mind presumes, for his own good and ours.   210
    HOR. I promised we would be contributors
And bear his charge of wooing, whatsoe'er.
    GRE. And so we will, provided that he win her.
    GRU. I would I were as sure of a good dinner.

207 *fear . . . bugs*] frighten boys with bugbears. Cf. *3 Hen. VI*, V,
  ii, 2 : " Warwick was a *bug* that *fear'd* us all."

[36]

Enter TRANIO *brave, and* BIONDELLO

TRA. Gentlemen, God save you.   If I may be bold,
Tell me, I beseech you, which is the readiest way
To the house of Signior Baptista Minola?

BION. He that has the two fair daughters: is 't he
you mean?

TRA. Even he, Biondello.   220

GRE. Hark you, sir; you mean not her to —

TRA. Perhaps, him and her, sir: what have you to do?

PET. Not her that chides, sir, at any hand, I pray.

TRA. I love no chiders, sir.   Biondello, let 's away.

LUC. Well begun, Tranio.

HOR.   Sir, a word ere you go;
Are you a suitor to the maid you talk of, yea or no?

TRA. And if I be, sir, is it any offence?

GRE. No; if without more words you will get you
                hence.

TRA. Why, sir, I pray, are not the streets as free
For me as for you?

GRE.   But so is not she.   230

TRA. For what reason, I beseech you?

GRE.   For this reason, if you 'll know,
That she 's the choice love of Signior Gremio.

HOR. That she 's the chosen of Signior Hortensio.

TRA. Softly, my masters! if you be gentlemen,
Do me this right; hear me with patience.
Baptista is a noble gentleman,
To whom my father is not all unknown;
And were his daughter fairer than she is,

[37]

She may more suitors have and me for one.
Fair Leda's daughter had a thousand wooers ; 240
Then well one more may fair Bianca have :
And so she shall ; Lucentio shall make one,
Though Paris came in hope to speed alone.

GRE. What, this gentleman will out-talk us all !

LUC. Sir, give him head : I know he'll prove a
jade.

PET. Hortensio, to what end are all these words ?

HOR. Sir, let me be so bold as ask you,
Did you yet ever see Baptista's daughter ?

TRA. No, sir ; but hear I do that he hath two,
The one as famous for a scolding tongue 250
As is the other for beauteous modesty.

PET. Sir, sir, the first's for me ; let her go by.

GRE. Yea, leave that labour to great Hercules ;
And let it be more than Alcides' twelve.

PET. Sir, understand you this of me in sooth :
The youngest daughter whom you hearken for
Her father keeps from all access of suitors ;
And will not promise her to any man
Until the elder sister first be wed :
The younger then is free and not before. 260

TRA. If it be so, sir, that you are the man
Must stead us all and me amongst the rest ;

---

245 *jade*] a horse that cannot be trusted. Cf. *Jul. Caes.*, IV, ii, 26–27 :
"Like *deceitful jades* Sink in the trial." Cotgrave translates
"gallier," a jade, a dull horse. See II, i, 200, *infra*.

256 *hearken for*] wait for, seek. Cf. *1 Hen. IV*, V, iv, 52 : "That
ever said I *hearken'd* for your death."

And if you break the ice and do this feat,
Achieve the elder, set the younger free
For our access, whose hap shall be to have her
Will not so graceless be to be ingrate.

HOR. Sir, you say well and well you do conceive;
And since you do profess to be a suitor,
You must, as we do, gratify this gentleman,
To whom we all rest generally beholding.   270

TRA. Sir, I shall not be slack: in sign whereof,
Please ye we may contrive this afternoon,
And quaff carouses to our mistress' health,
And do as adversaries do in law,
Strive mightily, but eat and drink as friends.

GRU. BION. O excellent motion! Fellows, let's be
     gone.

HOR. The motion's good indeed and be it so,
Petruchio, I shall be your ben venuto.   [*Exeunt.*

---

263 *feat*] Rowe's emendation of the original reading *seeke.*
272 *contrive*] spend. Cf. Spenser's *Faery Queen*, II, ix, 48, 5 : "Three
   ages, such as mortal men *contrive.*"

ACT SECOND — SCENE I — PADUA

A ROOM IN BAPTISTA'S HOUSE

Enter KATHARINA *and* BIANCA

BIANCA

OOD SISTER, WRONG me not, nor wrong yourself,
To make a bondmaid and a slave of me ;
That I disdain : but for these other gawds,
Unbind my hands, I 'll pull them off myself,
Yea, all my raiment, to my petticoat ;
Or what you will command me will I do,
So well I know my duty to my elders.

KATH. Of all thy suitors, here I charge thee, tell
Whom thou lovest best : see thou dissemble not.

---

3 *for these other gawds*] as for these other toys, trifles, trifling ornaments. Theobald substituted *gawds* for the original reading
goods, i. c. possessions. Neither reading is very pointed.

[40]

BIAN. Believe me, sister, of all the men alive   10
I never yet beheld that special face
Which I could fancy more than any other.
    KATH. Minion, thou liest. Is 't not Hortensio?
    BIAN. If you affect him, sister, here I swear
I 'll plead for you myself, but you shall have him.
    KATH. O then, belike, you fancy riches more:
You will have Gremio to keep you fair.
    BIAN. Is it for him you do envy me so?
Nay then you jest, and now I well perceive
You have but jested with me all this while: 20
I prithee, sister Kate, untie my hands.
    KATH. If that be jest, then all the rest was so.
                              [Strikes her.

              Enter BAPTISTA

    BAP. Why, how now, dame! whence grows this
          insolence?
Bianca, stand aside. Poor girl! she weeps.
Go ply thy needle; meddle not with her.
For shame, thou hilding of a devilish spirit,
Why dost thou wrong her that did ne'er wrong thee?
When did she cross thee with a bitter word?
    KATH. Her silence flouts me, and I 'll be revenged.
                         [Flies after Bianca.
    BAP. What, in my sight? Bianca, get thee in.   30
                          [Exit Bianca.
    KATH. What, will you not suffer me? Nay, now I
          see
She is your treasure, she must have a husband;

[41]

I must dance bare-foot on her wedding day
And for your love to her lead apes in hell.
Talk not to me: I will go sit and weep
Till I can find occasion of revenge. [*Exit.*

BAP. Was ever gentleman thus grieved as I?
But who comes here?

Enter GREMIO, LUCENTIO *in the habit of a mean man;* PETRUCHIO,
with HORTENSIO *as a musician; and* TRANIO, *with* BIONDELLO
bearing a lute and books

GRE. Good morrow, neighbour Baptista.

BAP. Good morrow, neighbour Gremio. God save 40
you, gentlemen!

PET. And you, good sir; Pray, have you not a
daughter
Call'd Katharina, fair and virtuous?

BAP. I have a daughter, sir, called Katharina.

GRE. You are too blunt: go to it orderly.

PET. You wrong me, Signior Gremio: give me leave.
I am a gentleman of Verona, sir,
That, hearing of her beauty and her wit,
Her affability and bashful modesty,
Her wondrous qualities and mild behaviour, 50
Am bold to show myself a forward guest
Within your house, to make mine eye the witness
Of that report which I so oft have heard.
And, for an entrance to my entertainment,
I do present you with a man of mine, [*Presenting Hortensio.*

34 *lead apes in hell*] The proverbial destiny of old maids and childless
women.

Cunning in music and the mathematics,
To instruct her fully in those sciences,
Whereof I know she is not ignorant:
Accept of him, or else you do me wrong:
His name is Licio, born in Mantua.   60
    BAP. You're welcome, sir; and he, for your good
        sake.
But for my daughter Katharine, this I know,
She is not for your turn, the more my grief.
    PET. I see you do not mean to part with her,
Or else you like not of my company.
    BAP. Mistake me not; I speak but as I find.
Whence are you, sir? what may I call your name?
    PET. Petruchio is my name; Antonio's son,
A man well known throughout all Italy.
    BAP. I know him well: you are welcome for his
        sake.   70
    GRE. Saving your tale, Petruchio, I pray,
Let us, that are poor petitioners, speak too:
Baccare! you are marvellous forward.
    PET. O, pardon me, Signior Gremio; I would fain be
        doing.
    GRE. I doubt it not, sir; but you will curse your
        wooing.
Neighbour, this is a gift very grateful, I am sure of
it. To express the like kindness, myself, that have been

---

73 *Baccare!*] A cant interjection formed from "back" or "back-
    wards." It is usually met with in the proverbial phrase "Backare,
    quod Mortimer to his sow." See John Heywood's *Epigrams*,
    and *Ralph Roister Doister*, I, 2.

more kindly beholding to you than any, freely give unto
you this young scholar [*presenting Lucentio*], that hath been
long studying at Rheims; as cunning in Greek, Latin, 90
and other languages, as the other in music and mathematics: his name is Cambio; pray, accept his service.

BAP. A thousand thanks, Signior Gremio. Welcome,
good Cambio. But, gentle sir [*to Tranio*], methinks you
walk like a stranger: may I be so bold to know the
cause of your coming?

TRA. Pardon me, sir, the boldness is mine own;
That, being a stranger in this city here,
Do make myself a suitor to your daughter,
Unto Bianca, fair and virtuous.
Nor is your firm resolve unknown to me,
In the preferment of the eldest sister.
This liberty is all that I request,
That, upon knowledge of my parentage,
I may have welcome 'mongst the rest that woo
And free access and favour as the rest:
And, toward the education of your daughters,
I here bestow a simple instrument,
And this small packet of Greek and Latin books:
If you accept them, then their worth is great. 100

BAP. Lucentio is your name; of whence, I pray?

TRA. Of Pisa, sir; son to Vincentio.

BAP. A mighty man of Pisa; by report
I know him well: you are very welcome, sir.
Take you the lute, and you the set of books;

---

101 *Lucentio . . . name*] Baptista probably learns Lucentio's name in
private talk with Tranio, after his last speech.

You shall go see your pupils presently.
Holla, within !

Enter a Servant

Sirrah, lead these gentlemen
To my daughters ; and tell them both,
These are their tutors : bid them use them well.

[*Exit Servant, with Luc. and Hor., Bio. following.*

We will go walk a little in the orchard,   110
And then to dinner.   You are passing welcome,
And so I pray you all to think yourselves.

PET. Signior Baptista, my business asketh haste,
And every day I cannot come to woo.
You knew my father well, and in him me,
Left solely heir to all his lands and goods,
Which I have better'd rather than decreased :
Then tell me, if I get your daughter's love,
What dowry shall I have with her to wife ?

BAP. After my death the one half of my lands,   120
And in possession twenty thousand crowns.

PET. And, for that dowry, I 'll assure her of
Her widowhood, be it that she survive me,
In all my lands and leases whatsoever :

---

114 *every day . . . to woo*] The line echoes the burden of a popular contemporary ballad called *The Ingenious Braggadocio* : " And I cannot
come every day to woo."   Puttenham quotes a similar line (" I cannot come a wooing every day ") from an interlude by himself called
"The Woer"; cf. *Arte of English Poesie* (1589), p. 213 (ed. Arber).
For other popular songs cited by Petruchio, see line 316, *infra :*
"We will be married o' Sunday," and IV, i, 124 and 129–130.

123 *widowhood*] the dower or jointure of a widow.

Let specialties be therefore drawn between us,
That covenants may be kept on either hand.

BAP. Ay, when the special thing is well obtain'd,
That is, her love; for that is all in all.

PET. Why, that is nothing; for I tell you, father,
I am as peremptory as she proud-minded;   130
And where two raging fires meet together
They do consume the thing that feeds their fury:
Though little fire grows great with little wind,
Yet extreme gusts will blow out fire and all:
So I to her and so she yields to me;
For I am rough and woo not like a babe.

BAP. Well mayst thou woo, and happy be thy speed!
But be thou arm'd for some unhappy words.

PET. Ay, to the proof; as mountains are for winds,
That shake not, though they blow perpetually.   140

Re-enter HORTENSIO, *with his head broke*

BAP. How now, my friend! why dost thou look so
　　　　pale?

HOR. For fear, I promise you, if I look pale.

BAP. What, will my daughter prove a good musician?

HOR. I think she 'll sooner prove a soldier:
Iron may hold with her, but never lutes.

BAP. Why, then thou canst not break her to the lute?

HOR. Why, no; for she hath broke the lute to me.
I did but tell her she mistook her frets,
And bow'd her hand to teach her fingering;
When, with a most impatient devilish spirit,   150

"Frets, call you these?" quoth she; " I 'll fume with them:"
And, with that word, she struck me on the head,
And through the instrument my pate made way ;
And there I stood amazed for a while,
As on a pillory, looking through the lute ;
While she did call me rascal fiddler
And twangling Jack ; with twenty such vile terms,
As had she studied to misuse me so.

   PET. Now, by the world, it is a lusty wench ;
I love her ten times more than e'er I did :   160
O, how I long to have some chat with her !

   BAP. Well, go with me and be not so discomfited :
Proceed in practice with my younger daughter ;
She 's apt to learn and thankful for good turns.
Signior Petruchio, will you go with us,
Or shall I send my daughter Kate to you ?

   PET. I pray you do ; I will attend her here,
      [*Exeunt Baptista, Gremio, Tranio, and Hortensio.*
And woo her with some spirit when she comes.
Say that she rail ; why then I 'll tell her plain
She sings as sweetly as a nightingale :   170

---

151 *Frets . . . fume*] "To fret and fume" is a very common expres-
    sion, meaning "to get angry."   The quibble on "fret," which also
    means "the stop of a guitar," is repeated in *Hamlet*, III, ii, 362 :
    "Though you can *fret* me, Yet you cannot play upon me."
157 *twangling Jack*] strumming fool. Cf. *Tempest*, III, ii, 146, " *twan-
    gling* instruments."   For this reproachful use of " Jack " cf. 280,
    infra, " swearing *Jack*."
169–173 *Say that she rail, etc.*] These lines, with a good many verbal
    alterations, were set to music by Sir Henry Bishop in a very
    popular song entitled "Should he upbraid."

[47]

Say that she frown ; I 'll say she looks as clear
As morning roses newly wash'd with dew :
Say she be mute and will not speak a word ;
Then I 'll commend her volubility,
And say she uttereth piercing eloquence :
If she do bid me pack, I 'll give her thanks,
As though she bid me stay by her a week :
If she deny to wed, I 'll crave the day
When I shall ask the banns, and when be married.
But here she comes ; and now, Petruchio, speak.   180

Enter KATHARINA

Good morrow, Kate ; for that 's your name, I hear.
   KATH. Well have you heard, but something hard of
         hearing :
They call me Katharine that do talk of me.
   PET. You lie, in faith ; for you are call'd plain Kate,
And bonny Kate, and sometimes Kate the curst ;
But Kate, the prettiest Kate in Christendom,
Kate of Kate-Hall, my super-dainty Kate,
For dainties are all Kates, and therefore, Kate,
Take this of me, Kate of my consolation ;
Hearing thy mildness praised in every town,   190
Thy virtues spoke of, and thy beauty sounded,
Yet not so deeply as to thee belongs,
Myself am moved to woo thee for my wife.
   KATH. Moved ! in good time : let him that moved
         you hither
Remove you hence : I knew you at the first
You were a moveable.

PET.   Why, what's a moveable?

KATH. A join'd-stool.

PET.   Thou hast hit it: come, sit on me.

KATH. Asses are made to bear, and so are you.

PET. Women are made to bear, and so are you.

KATH. No such jade as you, if me you mean.   200

PET. Alas, good Kate, I will not burden thee!
For, knowing thee to be but young and light, —

KATH. Too light for such a swain as you to catch;
And yet as heavy as my weight should be.

PET. Should be! should — buzz!

KATH.   Well ta'en, and like a buzzard.

PET. O slow-wing'd turtle! shall a buzzard take
         thee?

KATH. Ay, for a turtle, as he takes a buzzard.

PET. Come, come, you wasp; i' faith, you are too
         angry.

KATH. If I be waspish, best beware my sting.

PET. My remedy is then, to pluck it out.   210

KATH. Ay, if the fool could find it where it lies.

PET. Who knows not where a wasp does wear his
sting? In his tail.

KATH. In his tongue.

PET.   Whose tongue?

KATH. Yours, if you talk of tails: and so farewell.

---

197 *A join'd-stool*] A stool in moveable parts, which admitted of its
being folded up. For the proverbial phrase of mock apology, "I
took you for a *joint-stool*," see *Lear*, III, vi, 51.
200 *No such jade*] See note on I, ii, 256, *supra.*

PET. What, with my tongue in your tail? nay, come
      again,
Good Kate; I am a gentleman.
KATH.   That I 'll try.   [*She strikes him.*
PET. I swear I 'll cuff you, if you strike again.
KATH. So may you lose your arms:
If you strike me, you are no gentleman;
And if no gentleman, why then no arms.   220
  PET. A herald, Kate? O, put me in thy books!
KATH. What is your crest? a coxcomb?
PET. A combless cock, so Kate will be my hen.
KATH. No cock of mine; you crow too like a craven.
PET. Nay, come, Kate, come; you must not look so
      sour.
KATH. It is my fashion, when I see a crab.
PET. Why, here's no crab; and therefore look not sour.
KATH. There is, there is.
PET. Then show it me.
KATH.   Had I a glass, I would.
PET. What, you mean my face?
KATH.   Well aim'd of such a young one.   230
PET. Now, by Saint George, I am too young for you.
KATH. Yet you are wither'd.
PET.   'T is with cares.
KATH.   I care not.

---

221 *put me in thy books*] a quibble on the two senses of the phrase, viz.,
"taking one into favour," or "putting one in one's good books,"
and "enrolling one's name in the registers (of the Herald's
College)." Cf. *Much Ado*, I, i, 63: "I see, lady, the gentleman is
not *in your books*."

PET. Nay, hear you, Kate: in sooth you scape not so.
KATH. I chafe you, if I tarry: let me go.
PET. No, not a whit: I find you passing gentle.
'T was told me you were rough and coy and sullen,
And now I find report a very liar;
For thou art pleasant, gamesome, passing courteous,
But slow in speech, yet sweet as spring-time flowers:
Thou canst not frown, thou canst not look askance,   240
Nor bite the lip, as angry wenches will,
Nor hast thou pleasure to be cross in talk,
But thou with mildness entertain'st thy wooers,
With gentle conference, soft and affable.
Why does the world report that Kate doth limp?
O slanderous world! Kate like the hazel-twig
Is straight and slender, and as brown in hue
As hazel-nuts and sweeter than the kernels.
O, let me see thee walk: thou dost not halt.
  KATH. Go, fool, and whom thou keep'st command.   250
  PET. Did ever Dian so become a grove
As Kate this chamber with her princely gait?
O, be thou Dian, and let her be Kate;
And then let Kate be chaste and Dian sportful!
  KATH. Where did you study all this goodly speech?
PET. It is extempore, from my mother-wit.
KATH. A witty mother! witless else her son.
PET. Am I not wise?
KATH.   Yes; keep you warm.

---

258 *keep you warm*] an adaptation of some such proverbial platitude as
   "A wise man keeps out of the cold." The expression reappears in
   Much Ado, I, i, 57: "If he have wit enough *to keep himself warm.*"

PET. Marry, so I mean, sweet Katharine, in thy bed :
And therefore, setting all this chat aside,   260
Thus in plain terms : your father hath consented
That you shall be my wife ; your dowry 'greed on ;
And, will you, nill you, I will marry you.
Now, Kate, I am a husband for your turn ;
For, by this light, whereby I see thy beauty,
Thy beauty, that doth make me like thee well,
Thou must be married to no man but me ;
For I am he am born to tame you Kate,
And bring you from a wild Kate to a Kate
Conformable as other household Kates.   270
Here comes your father : never make denial ;
I must and will have Katharine to my wife.

Re-enter BAPTISTA, GREMIO, *and* TRANIO

BAP. Now, Signior Petruchio, how speed you with
        my daughter ?
PET. How but well, sir ? how but well ?
It were impossible I should speed amiss.
BAP. Why, how now, daughter Katharine ! in your
        dumps ?
KATH. Call you me daughter ? now, I promise you
You have show'd a tender fatherly regard,
To wish me wed to one half lunatic ;
A mad-cap ruffian and a swearing Jack,   280
That thinks with oaths to face the matter out.
PET. Father, 't is thus : yourself and all the world,
That talk'd of her, have talk'd amiss of her :

280 *swearing Jack*] Cf. II, i, 157, *supra*, " twangling Jack."

If she be curst, it is for policy,
For she 's not froward, but modest as the dove ;
She is not hot, but temperate as the morn ;
For patience she will prove a second Grissel,
And Roman Lucrece for her chastity :
And to conclude, we have 'greed so well together,
That upon Sunday is the wedding-day.   290
    KATH. I 'll see thee hang'd on Sunday first.
    GRE. Hark, Petruchio ; she says she 'll see thee hang'd
        first.
    TRA. Is this your speeding ? nay, then, good night
        our part !
    PET. Be patient, gentlemen ; I choose her for myself :
If she and I be pleased, what 's that to you ?
'T is bargain'd 'twixt us twain, being alone,
That she shall still be curst in company.
I tell you, 't is incredible to believe
How much she loves me : O, the kindest Kate !
She hung about my neck ; and kiss on kiss   300
She vied so fast, protesting oath on oath,
That in a twink she won me to her love.
O, you are novices ! 't is a world to see,

---

287 *Grissel*] Griselda was the recognised type of patience in women.
Her story, as told by Petrarch after Boccaccio, was reproduced in
Chaucer's *Canterbury Tales*, and on it was based the play of *The
Patient Grissel*, by Haughton, Chettle and Dekker (1603).
293 *our part*] our part of the bargain.
301 *She vied*] She vied with me in giving, she bid in competition with
me. Cf. out-vied, *i. e.* outbid, line 377, *infra*.
303 *a world to see*] a wonderful sight ; a common Elizabethan
expression.

How tame, when men and women are alone,
A meacock wretch can make the curstest shrew.
Give me thy hand, Kate : I will unto Venice,
To buy apparel 'gainst the wedding-day.
Provide the feast, father, and bid the guests ;
I will be sure my Katherine shall be fine.
    BAP. I know not what to say : but give me your
              hands ;   310
God send you joy, Petruchio ! 't is a match.
    GRE. TRA. Amen, say we : we will be witnesses.
    PET. Father, and wife, and gentlemen, adieu
I will to Venice ; Sunday comes apace :
We will have rings, and things, and fine array ,
And, kiss me, Kate, we will be married o' Sunday.
                [*Exeunt Petruchio and Katharina severally.*
    GRE. Was ever match clapp'd up so suddenly ?
    BAP. Faith, gentlemen, now I play a merchant's part,
And venture madly on a desperate mart.
    TRA. 'T was a commodity lay fretting by you :   320
'T will bring you gain, or perish on the seas.
    BAP. The gain I seek is, quiet in the match.
    GRE. No doubt but he hath got a quiet catch.
But now, Baptista, to your younger daughter :

---

305 *meacock*] spiritless. Cotgrave's *French-English Dict.* gives "milk-
    sop," and "worthless fellow" as synonyms for "a meacock."
316 *we will be married o' Sunday*] In *Ralph Roister Doister*, V, 6, the old
    song is given, with the refrain (thrice repeated) "I mun be married
    a Sunday." Petruchio quotes other old songs at line 114, *supra*,
    and at IV, i, 124 and 129–130, *infra*.
323 *got a quiet catch*] made a safe haul.

Now is the day we long have looked for :
I am your neighbour, and was suitor first.
   TRA. And I am one that love Bianca more
Than words can witness, or your thoughts can guess.
   GRE. Youngling, thou canst not love so dear as I.
   TRA. Greybeard, thy love doth freeze.
   GRE.   But thine doth fry.
Skipper, stand back : 't is age that nourisheth.   331
   TRA. But youth in ladies' eyes that flourisheth.
   BAP. Content you, gentlemen : I will compound this
          strife :
'T is deeds must win the prize ; and he, of both,
That can assure my daughter greatest dower
Shall have my Bianca's love.
Say, Signior Gremio, what can you assure her ?
   GRE. First, as you know, my house within the city
Is richly furnished with plate and gold ;
Basins and ewers to lave her dainty hands ;   340
My hangings all of Tyrian tapestry ;
In ivory coffers I have stuff'd my crowns ;
In cypress chests my arras counterpoints,
Costly apparel, tents, and canopies,
Fine linen, Turkey cushions boss'd with pearl,
Valance of Venice gold in needlework,
Pewter and brass and all things that belong
To house or housekeeping : then, at my farm

---

344 *tents, and canopies*] bed hangings.
345 *boss'd*] studded.
346 *Valance . . . needlework*] Drapery of the bedstead made of Venetian lace in gold thread.

[55]

I have a hundred milch-kine to the pail,
Sixscore fat oxen standing in my stalls, 350
And all things answerable to this portion.
Myself am struck in years, I must confess;
And if I die to-morrow, this is hers,
If whilst I live she will be only mine.

TRA. That "only" came well in. Sir, list to me:
I am my father's heir and only son:
If I may have your daughter to my wife,
I 'll leave her houses three or four as good,
Within rich Pisa walls, as any one
Old Signior Gremio has in Padua; 360
Besides two thousand ducats by the year
Of fruitful land, all which shall be her jointure.
What, have I pinch'd you, Signior Gremio?

GRE. Two thousand ducats by the year of land!
My land amounts not to so much in all:
That she shall have; besides an argosy
That now is lying in Marseilles' road.
What, have I choked you with an argosy?

TRA. Gremio, 't is known my father hath no less
Than three great argosies; besides two galliasses, 370
And twelve tight galleys: these I will assure her,
And twice as much, whate'er thou offer'st next.

GRE. Nay, I have offer'd all, I have no more;
And she can have no more than all I have:
If you like me, she shall have me and mine.

---

349 *milch-kine to the pail*] cows for milking.
363 *pinch'd*] got the better of, hurt.

TRA. Why, then the maid is mine from all the world,
By your firm promise: Gremio is out-vied.
    BAP. I must confess your offer is the best;
And, let your father make her the assurance,
She is your own; else, you must pardon me,   380
If you should die before him, where's her dower?
    TRA. That's but a cavil: he is old, I young.
    GRE. And may not young men die, as well as old?
    BAP. Well, gentlemen,
I am thus resolved: on Sunday next you know
My daughter Katharine is to be married:
Now, on the Sunday following, shall Bianca
Be bride to you, if you make this assurance;
If not, to Signior Gremio:
And so, I take my leave, and thank you both.   390
    GRE. Adieu, good neighbour.   [Exit Baptista.
                           Now I fear thee not:
Sirrah young gamester, your father were a fool
To give thee all, and in his waning age
Set foot under thy table: tut, a toy!
An old Italian fox is not so kind, my boy.   [Exit.
    TRA. A vengeance on your crafty wither'd hide!
Yet I have faced it with a card of ten.
'Tis in my head to do my master good:

---

377 *out-vied*] out-bid; see line 301, *supra*.
388 *if . . . assurance*] if you give this security.
397 *a card of ten*] a card of ten spots, which might, when skilfully
    played, count highest in "primero" and other contemporary games.
    Cf. Day's *Law tricks* (1608) Act V: "I may be outfaced of myself,
    with *a card of ten*."

I see no reason but supposed Lucentio
Must get a father, call'd — supposed Vincentio;   44
And that's a wonder : fathers commonly
Do get their children ; but in this case of wooing,
A child shall get a sire, if I fail not of my cunning. [*Exit.*

ACT THIRD — SCENE I — PADUA

BAPTISTA'S HOUSE

Enter LUCENTIO, HORTENSIO, *and* BIANCA

LUCENTIO

IDDLER, FORBEAR;
you grow too forward, sir:
Have you so soon forgot the
entertainment
Her sister Katharine welcomed
you withal?

HOR. But, wrangling pedant,
this is
The patroness of heavenly harmony:
Then give me leave to have
prerogative;
And when in music we have
spent an hour,

Your lecture shall have leisure for as much.

LUC. Preposterous ass, that never read so far
To know the cause why music was ordain'd!   10
Was it not to refresh the mind of man

[59]

After his studies or his usual pain?
Then give me leave to read philosophy,
And while I pause, serve in your harmony.

HOR. Sirrah, I will not bear these braves of thine.

BIAN. Why, gentlemen, you do me double wrong,
To strive for that which resteth in my choice:
I am no breeching scholar in the schools;
I 'll not be tied to hours nor 'pointed times,
But learn my lessons as I please myself.   20
And, to cut off all strife, here sit we down:
Take you your instrument, play you the whiles;
His lecture will be done ere you have tuned.

HOR. You 'll leave his lecture when I am in tune?

LUC. That will be never: tune your instrument.

BIAN. Where left we last?

LUC. Here, madam:
    " Hic ibat Simois; hic est Sigeia tellus;
        Hic steterat Priami regia celsa senis."

BIAN. Construe them.   30

LUC. "Hic ibat," as I told you before, — "Simois,"
I am Lucentio, — "hic est," son unto Vincentio of Pisa,
— "Sigeia tellus," disguised thus to get your love; —
" Hic steterat," and that Lucentio that comes a-wooing,

---

12 *his usual pain*] his customary toil.

18 *breeching scholar*] a boy, fit to be breeched or flogged. " A breeching boy " is common in the same sense.

28-29 *Hic ibat, etc.*] From Ovid's *Heroides*, I, 33, 34. Ovid is causing
   a Greek soldier to paint with wine on a table the disposition of
   the opposing armies at Troy. The line reads in Ovid: " *Hac* ibat
   Simois, *haec* est Sigeia tellus."

— "Priami," is my man Tranio, — "regia," bearing my
port, — "celsa senis," that we might beguile the old
pantaloon.

HOR. Madam, my instrument's in tune.

BIAN. Let's hear. O fie! the treble jars.

LUC. Spit in the hole, man, and tune again.

BIAN. Now let me see if I can construe it: 40
"Hic ibat Simois," I know you not, — "hic est Sigeia
tellus," I trust you not, — "Hic steterat Priami," take
heed he hear us not, — "regia," presume not, — "celsa
senis," despair not.

HOR. Madam, 't is now in tune.

LUC.   All but the base.

HOR. The base is right; 't is the base knave that
          jars.

[*Aside*] How fiery and forward our pedant is!
Now, for my life, the knave doth court my love:
Pedascule, I 'll watch you better yet.

BIAN. In time I may believe, yet I mistrust.

LUC. Mistrust it not; for, sure, Æacides   50
Was Ajax, call'd so from his grandfather.

BIAN. I must believe my master; else, I promise
          you,
I should be arguing still upon that doubt:
But let it rest. Now, Licio, to you:
Good masters, take it not unkindly, pray,
That I have been thus pleasant with you both.

---

36 *the old pantaloon*] Cf. *supra*, I, i, 47, note.

48 *Pedascule*] Apparently a contemptuous diminutive of "pedant."
   No other example of the word is found.

HOR. You may go walk, and give me leave a while:
My lessons make no music in three parts.

LUC. Are you so formal, sir? well, I must wait,
[*Aside*] And watch withal; for, but I be deceived,   60
Our fine musician groweth amorous.

HOR. Madam, before you touch the instrument,
To learn the order of my fingering,
I must begin with rudiments of art;
To teach you gamut in a briefer sort,
More pleasant, pithy, and effectual,
Than hath been taught by any of my trade:
And there it is in writing, fairly drawn.

BIAN. Why, I am past my gamut long ago.

HOR. Yet read the gamut of Hortensio.   70

BIAN. [*reads*] "'Gamut' I am, the ground of all accord,
          'A re,' to plead Hortensio's passion;
      'B mi,' Bianca, take him for thy lord,
          'C fa ut,' that loves with all affection:
      'D sol re,' one clef, two notes have I:
          'E la mi,' show pity, or I die."

Call you this gamut? tut, I like it not:
Old fashions please me best; I am not so nice,
To change true rules for old inventions.

---

65 *gamut*] the scale in music. The word is derived from "gamma,"
the name of the letter "g" in Greek, after which the lowest note
in the musical scale was called. Cf. *Pathway to Music* (1596):
"It is needfull for him that will learne to sing truely, to understand
his Scale, or (as they commonly call it) the *Gamma ut*."

79 *change . . . inventions*] The Second Folio substituted *change* for the

[62]

Enter a Servant

SERV. Mistress, your father prays you leave your
    books,   80
And help to dress your sister's chamber up :
You know to-morrow is the wedding-day.
   BIAN. Farewell, sweet masters both ; I must be gone.
                               [Exeunt Bianca and Servant.
   LUC. Faith, mistress, then I have no cause to stay.
                                     [Exit.
   HOR. But I have cause to pry into this pedant :
Methinks he looks as though he were in love :
Yet if thy thoughts, Bianca, be so humble,
To cast thy wandering eyes on every stale,
Seize thee that list : if once I find thee ranging,
Hortensio will be quit with thee by changing.   *[Exit.* 90

SCENE II—PADUA

BEFORE BAPTISTA'S HOUSE

Enter BAPTISTA, GREMIO, TRANIO, KATHARINA, BIANCA, LUCENTIO,
and others, attendants

BAP. Signior Lucentio [*To Tranio*], this is the 'pointed
    day.
That Katharine and Petruchio should be married,

---

charge of the First Folio, which was an obvious misprint ; *old* was
altered unnecessarily by Theobald to *odd*, an alteration which has
been very widely adopted.

And yet we hear not of our son-in-law.
What will be said? what mockery will it be,
To want the bridegroom when the priest attends
To speak the ceremonial rites of marriage!
What says Lucentio to this shame of ours?

    KATH. No shame but mine: I must, forsooth, be
        forced
To give my hand, opposed against my heart,
Unto a mad-brain rudesby, full of spleen;   10
Who woo'd in haste, and means to wed at leisure.
I told you, I, he was a frantic fool,
Hiding his bitter jests in blunt behaviour:
And, to be noted for a merry man,
He 'll woo a thousand, 'point the day of marriage,
Make friends, invite, and proclaim the banns;
Yet never means to wed where he hath woo'd.
Now must the world point at poor Katharine,
And say, "Lo, there is mad Petruchio's wife,
If it would please him come and marry her!"   20

    TRA. Patience, good Katharine, and Baptista too.
Upon my life, Petruchio means but well,
Whatever fortune stays him from his word:
Though he be blunt, I know him passing wise;
Though he be merry, yet withal he 's honest.

    KATH. Would Katharine had never seen him though!
        [*Exit weeping, followed by Bianca and others.*

---

10 *rudesby, full of spleen*] a ruffian, full of caprice, whimsical. Cf.
   1 Hen. IV, V, ii, 19: "A *harebrain'd* Hotspur, govern'd by a
   spleen."

BAP. Go, girl ; I cannot blame thee now to weep ;
For such an injury would vex a very saint,
Much more a shrew of thy impatient humour.

Enter BIONDELLO

BION. Master, master ! news, old news, and such so
news as you never heard of !
BAP. Is it new and old too ? how may that be ?
BION. Why, is it not news, to hear of Petruchio's
coming ?
BAP. Is he come ?
BION. Why, no, sir.
BAP. What then ?
BION. He is coming.
BAP. When will he be here ?
BION. When he stands where I am and sees you there.
TRA. But say, what to thine old news ?   40
BION. Why, Petruchio is coming in a new hat and
an old jerkin, a pair of old breeches thrice turned, a
pair of boots that have been candle-cases, one buckled,
another laced, an old rusty sword ta'en out of the town-
armoury, with a broken hilt, and chapeless ; with two
broken points : his horse hipped with an old mothy sad-
dle and stirrups of no kindred ; besides, possessed with
the glanders and like to mose in the chine ; troubled

43 *candle-cases*] boxes to keep candles in.
46 *horse hipped*] This list of diseases in horses is conceived in a
Rabelaisian vein. There is no good ground for doubting, with
some critics, Shakespeare's responsibility for it.

with the lampass, infected with the fashions, full of
windgalls, sped with spavins, rayed with the yellows, *so*
past cure of the fives, stark spoiled with the staggers,
begnawn with the bots, swayed in the back and shoulder-
shotten; near-legged before and with a half-cheeked bit
and a head-stall of sheep's leather which, being restrained
to keep him from stumbling, hath been often burst and
now repaired with knots; one girth six times pieced and
a woman's crupper of velure, which hath two letters for
her name fairly set down in studs, and here and there
pieced with pack-thread.

BAP. Who comes with him?   *60*

BION. O, sir, his lackey, for all the world caparisoned
like the horse; with a linen stock on one leg, and a
kersey boot-hose on the other, gartered with a red and
blue list; an old hat, and " the humour of forty fancies "

---

49 *fashions*] A corruption of the French word " farcin," a disease in
   horses. Cf. Dekker's *Guls Hornbook* (1609) : " *Fashions* was then
   counted a disease, and horses died of it."

51 *fives*] " Fives," like " fashions " is a corruption of a French word.
   The disease, which is correctly known as " avives " or " vives," is
   an inflammation of the glands of the ear.

64 " *humour of forty fancies* "] The inverted commas are not found in
   the First Folio; they appear in the Quarto reprint of 1631.
   Petruchio's hat was adorned with a whimsical knot of ribbons.
   " Fancies " was applied to a bundle of ribbons of variegated colour.
   Peacham in his *Worth of a Penny* describes " a weather-beaten
   fancy worn (in a hat) ' for fashion's sake.' " Cf. Brome's *Mad
   Couple* (1652), Prologue : " I 've a new Suite, And Ribbons fashion-
   able, yclipt *Fancies*." Sir John Davies in his *Epigrams* (1598) re-
   fuses to follow the manner of the desperate lover and " some pied

pricked in 't for a feather : a monster, a very monster in
apparel, and not like a Christian footboy or a gentleman's
lackey.

TRA. 'T is some odd humour pricks him to this fashion ;
Yet oftentimes he goes but mean-apparell'd.

BAP. I am glad he 's come, howsoe'er he comes.   70

BION. Why, sir, he comes not.

BAP. Didst thou not say he comes ?

BION. Who ? that Petruchio came ?

BAP. Ay, that Petruchio came.

BION. No, sir ; I say his horse comes, with him on
his back.

BAP. Why, that 's all one.

BION. Nay, by Saint Jamy,
    I hold you a penny,
    A horse and a man   80
    Is more than one,
    And yet not many.

Enter PETRUCHIO *and* GRUMIO

PET. Come, where be these gallants ? who 's at
        home ?

BAP. You are welcome, sir.

PET.   And yet I come not well.

BAP. And yet you halt not.

---

colours in my bonnet stick." " Fancy-work " and " fancy dress "
are expressions of a cognate significance. " The humour of forty
fancies " resembles the title of contemporary song-books. Cf.
Thomas Ravenscroft's " Melismata : Musical *Phancies* fitting the
Court, Citie and Country *Humours*," 1611.

TRA.   Not so well apparell'd
As I wish you were.
    PET.   Were it better, I should rush in thus.
But where is Kate? where is my lovely bride?
How does my father?   Gentles, methinks you frown:
And wherefore gaze this goodly company,   90
As if they saw some wondrous monument,
Some comet or unusual prodigy?
    BAP. Why, sir, you know this is your wedding-
          day:
First were we sad, fearing you would not come;
Now sadder, that you come so unprovided.
Fie, doff this habit, shame to your estate,
An eye-sore to our solemn festival!
    TRA. And tell us, what occasion of import
Hath all so long detain'd you from your wife,
And sent you hither so unlike yourself?   100
    PET. Tedious it were to tell, and harsh to hear:
Sufficeth, I am come to keep my word,
Though in some part enforced to digress;
Which, at more leisure, I will so excuse
As you shall well be satisfied withal.
But where is Kate?   I stay too long from her:
The morning wears, 't is time we were at church.
    TRA. See not your bride in these unreverent robes:
Go to my chamber; put on clothes of mine.
    PET. Not I, believe me: thus I 'll visit her.   110
    BAP. But thus, I trust, you will not marry her.

---

103 *digress*] deviate from my promised action.

[68]

PET. Good sooth, even thus ; therefore ha' done with
          words :
To me she 's married, not unto my clothes :
Could I repair what she will wear in me,
As I can change these poor accoutrements,
'T were well for Kate and better for myself.
But what a fool am I to chat with you,
When I should bid good morrow to my bride,
And seal the title with a lovely kiss !
                            [*Exeunt Petruchio and Grumio.*

TRA. He hath some meaning in his mad attire :   120
We will persuade him, be it possible,
To put on better ere he go to church.

BAP. I 'll after him, and see the event of this.
               [*Exeunt Baptista, Gremio, and attendants.*

TRA. But to her love concerneth us to add
Her father's liking : which to bring to pass,
As I before imparted to your worship,
I am to get a man, — whate'er he be,
It skills not much, we 'll fit him to our turn, —
And he shall be Vincentio of Pisa ;
And make assurance here in Padua   130
Of greater sums than I have promised.

---

114 *what . . . wear in me*] what she will wear out in me ; what worry
    she will cause me.
124 *But to her love . . . add*] The original reading is *But sir, Love,*
    which leaves the line defective. It is possible that "sir" is a
    misprint for "to her." The elliptical construction of a verb with-
    out any nominative is not uncommon in Elizabethan English.
    The meaning is, "It behoves us to add to her love her father's
    consent."

So shall you quietly enjoy your hope,
And marry sweet Bianca with consent.
    Luc. Were it not that my fellow-schoolmaster
Doth watch Bianca's steps so narrowly,
'T were good, methinks, to steal our marriage;
Which once perform'd, let all the world say no,
I 'll keep mine own, despite of all the world.
    Tra. That by degrees we mean to look into,
And watch our vantage in this business: 140
We 'll over-reach the greybeard, Gremio,
The narrow-prying father, Minola,
The quaint musician, amorous Licio;
All for my master's sake, Lucentio.

Re-enter Gremio

Signior Gremio, came you from the church?
    Gre. As willingly as e'er I came from school.
    Tra. And is the bride and bridegroom coming
        home?
    Gre. A bridegroom say you? 't is a groom indeed,
A grumbling groom, and that the girl shall find.
    Tra. Curster than she? why, 't is impossible.   150
    Gre. Why, he 's a devil, a devil, a very fiend.
    Tra. Why, she 's a devil, a devil, the devil's dam.
    Gre. Tut, she 's a lamb, a dove, a fool to him!
I 'll tell you, Sir Lucentio: when the priest
Should ask, if Katharine should be his wife,
"Ay, by gogs-wouns," quoth he; and swore so loud,

---

136 *steal our marriage*] make our marriage clandestine.

That, all amazed, the priest let fall the book ;
And, as he stoop'd again to take it up,
This mad-brain'd bridegroom took him such a cuff,
That down fell priest and book, and book and priest : 160
" Now take them up," quoth he, " if any list."
   TRA. What said the wench when he rose again ?
   GRE. Trembled and shook ; for why he stamp'd and
       swore,
As if the vicar meant to cozen him.
But after many ceremonies done,
He calls for wine : " A health ! " quoth he ; as if
He had been aboard, carousing to his mates
After a storm : quaff'd off the muscadel,
And threw the sops all in the sexton's face ;
Having no other reason   170
But that his beard grew thin and hungerly
And seem'd to ask him sops as he was drinking.
This done, he took the bride about the neck
And kiss'd her lips with such a clamorous smack
That at the parting all the church did echo :
And I seeing this came thence for very shame ;
And after me, I know, the rout is coming.
Such a mad marriage never was before :
Hark, hark ! I hear the minstrels play.   [Music.

163–179] This passage was printed as prose in the First Folio, but
   rightly appeared as verse in the Second Folio.
166 *He calls for wine*] It was the common practice to drink sweet
   wine, usually muscadel or muscadine, in church at the end of the
   wedding ceremony.

Re-enter PETRUCHIO, KATHARINA, BIANCA, BAPTISTA, HORTENSIO, GRUMIO, *and Train*

PET. Gentlemen and friends, I thank you for your
    pains : 180
I know you think to dine with me to-day,
And have prepared great store of wedding cheer ;
But so it is, my haste doth call me hence,
And therefore here I mean to take my leave.
  BAP. Is 't possible you will away to-night ?
  PET. I must away to-day, before night come :
Make it no wonder ; if you knew my business,
You would entreat me rather go than stay.
And, honest company, I thank you all,
That have beheld me give away myself 190
To this most patient, sweet, and virtuous wife :
Dine with my father, drink a health to me ;
For I must hence ; and farewell to you all.
  TRA. Let us entreat you stay till after dinner.
  PET. It may not be.
  GRE.   Let me entreat you.
  PET. It cannot be.
  KATH.   Let me entreat you.
  PET. I am content.
  KATH.   Are you content to stay ?
  PET. I am content you shall entreat me stay ;
But yet not stay, entreat me how you can.
  KATH. Now, if you love me, stay.
  PET.   Grumio, my horse. 200
  GRU. Ay, sir, they be ready : the oats have eaten the
horses.

KATH. Nay, then,
Do what thou canst, I will not go to-day;
No, nor to-morrow, not till I please myself.
The door is open, sir; there lies your way;
You may be jogging whiles your boots are green;
For me, I 'll not be gone till I please myself:
'T is like you 'll prove a jolly surly groom,
That take it on you at the first so roundly.   210

PET. O Kate, content thee; prithee, be not angry.

KATH. I will be angry: what hast thou to do?
Father, be quiet: he shall stay my leisure.

GRE. Ay, marry, sir, now it begins to work.

KATH. Gentlemen, forward to the bridal dinner:
I see a woman may be made a fool,
If she had not a spirit to resist.

PET. They shall go forward, Kate, at thy command.
Obey the bride, you that attend on her;
Go to the feast, revel and domineer,   220
Carouse full measure to her maidenhead,
Be mad and merry, or go hang yourselves:
But for my bonny Kate, she must with me.
Nay, look not big, nor stamp, nor stare, nor fret;
I will be master of what is mine own:
She is my goods, my chattels; she is my house,
My household stuff, my field, my barn,
My horse, my ox, my ass, my any thing;

---

207 *green*] fresh, new. The phrase "boots are green" seems to
have been proverbial.
210 *That . . . roundly*] That at the outset behave so bluntly, so in-
solently. Cf. note, *supra*, I, ii, 57.

[73]

And here she stands, touch her whoever dare;
I 'll bring mine action on the proudest he 230
That stops my way in Padua. Grumio,
Draw forth thy weapon, we are beset with thieves;
Rescue thy mistress, if thou be a man.
Fear not, sweet wench, they shall not touch thee, Kate:
I 'll buckler thee against a million.

[Exeunt Petruchio, Katharina, and Grumio.

BAP. Nay, let them go, a couple of quiet ones.
GRE. Went they not quickly, I should die with
laughing.
TRA. Of all mad matches never was the like.
LUC. Mistress, what 's your opinion of your sister?
BIAN. That, being mad herself, she 's madly mated. 240
GRE. I warrant him, Petruchio is Kated.
BAP. Neighbours and friends, though bride and bride-
groom wants
For to supply the places at the table,
You know there wants no junkets at the feast.
Lucentio, you shall supply the bridegroom's place;
And let Bianca take her sister's room.
TRA. Shall sweet Bianca practise how to bride it?
BAP. She shall, Lucentio. Come, gentlemen, let 's go.

[Exeunt.

240 *mated*] See note on *Com. of Errors*, III, ii, 54.

[74]

ACT FOURTH—SCENE I—PETRUCHIO'S COUNTRY HOUSE

Enter GRUMIO

GRUMIO

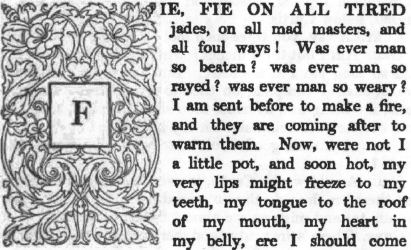

FIE, FIE ON ALL TIRED jades, on all mad masters, and all foul ways! Was ever man so beaten? was ever man so rayed? was ever man so weary? I am sent before to make a fire, and they are coming after to warm them. Now, were not I a little pot, and soon hot, my very lips might freeze to my teeth, my tongue to the roof of my mouth, my heart in my belly, ere I should come by a fire to thaw me: but I, with blowing the fire, shall warm myself; for, considering the weather, a taller man than I will take cold. Holla, ho! Curtis!

10

Enter CURTIS

CURT. Who is it that calls so coldly?

GRU. A piece of ice: if thou doubt it, thou mayst slide from my shoulder to my heel with no greater a run but my head and my neck. A fire, good Curtis.

CURT. Is my master and his wife coming, Grumio?

GRU. O, ay, Curtis, ay: and therefore fire, fire; cast on no water.

CURT. Is she so hot a shrew as she's reported?

GRU. She was, good Curtis, before this frost: but, thou knowest, winter tames man, woman, and beast; for it so hath tamed my old master, and my new mistress, and myself, fellow Curtis.

CURT. Away, you three-inch fool! I am no beast.

GRU. Am I but three inches? why, thy horn is a foot; and so long am I at the least. But wilt thou make a fire, or shall I complain on thee to our mistress, whose hand, she being now at hand, thou shalt soon feel, to thy cold comfort, for being slow in thy hot office?

CURT. I prithee, good Grumio, tell me, how goes the world? 30

GRU. A cold world, Curtis, in every office but thine; and therefore fire: do thy duty, and have thy duty; for my master and mistress are almost frozen to death.

CURT. There's fire ready; and therefore, good Grumio, the news.

16–17 *fire, fire* . . . *water*] a misquotation of the old popular catch, "Scotland burneth; Fire, fire, fire, fire. Cast on some more water."

GRU. Why, "Jack, boy! ho! boy!" and as much news as thou wilt.

CURT. Come, you are so full of cony-catching!

GRU. Why, therefore fire; for I have caught extreme cold. Where's the cook? is supper ready, the house 40 trimmed, rushes strewed, cobwebs swept; the serving-men in their new fustian, their white stockings, and every officer his wedding-garment on? Be the jacks fair within, the jills fair without, the carpets laid, and every thing in order?

CURT. All ready; and therefore, I pray thee, news.

GRU. First, know, my horse is tired; my master and
    mistress fallen out.

CURT. How?

GRU. Out of their saddles into the dirt; and thereby
    hangs a tale.   50

CURT. Let's ha't, good Grumio.

GRU. Lend thine ear.

CURT. Here.

GRU. There.   *[Strikes him.*

---

36 *"Jack, boy! ho! boy!"*] The first words of an old round or catch in three parts (given in Ravenscroft's *Pammelia,* 1609), of which the first words are "Jack boy! ho! boy! news; the cat is in the well."

41 *rushes strewed*] The floors of Elizabethan houses were usually covered with rushes in place of carpets.

43-44 *jacks fair . . . carpets laid*] Grumio quibbles on the words "jacks" and "jills," which were used for men-servants and maid-servants respectively, as well as for two kinds of drinking vessels — of leather and metal respectively. The carpets were the tablecloths.

[77]

CURT. This is to feel a tale, not to hear a tale.

GRU. And therefore 't is called a sensible tale: and this cuff was but to knock at your ear, and beseech listening. Now I begin: *Imprimis*, we came down a foul hill, my master riding behind my mistress, —

CURT. Both of one horse ?   60

GRU. What 's that to thee ?

CURT. Why, a horse.

GRU. Tell thou the tale : but hadst thou not crossed me, thou shouldst have heard how her horse fell and she under her horse ; thou shouldst have heard in how miry a place, how she was bemoiled, how he left her with the horse upon her, how he beat me because her horse stumbled, how she waded through the dirt to pluck him off me, how he swore, how she prayed, that never prayed before, how I cried, how the horses ran away, 70 how her bridle was burst, how I lost my crupper, with many things of worthy memory, which now shall die in oblivion and thou return unexperieneed to thy grave.

CURT. By this reckoning he is more shrew than she.

GRU. Ay; and that thou and the proudest of you all shall find when he comes home. But what talk I of this ? Call forth Nathaniel, Joseph, Nicholas, Philip, Walter, Sugarsop and the rest : let their heads be sleekly combed, their blue coats brushed, and their garters of an indifferent knit : let them curtsy with their 80 left legs, and not presume to touch a hair of my

---

79 *blue coats*] Blue was the ordinary colour of menservants' dress.
80 *indifferent knit*] ordinary texture, neither too fine nor too coarse.

master's horse-tail till they kiss their hands. Are they all ready?

CURT. They are.

GRU. Call them forth.

CURT. Do you hear, ho? you must meet my master to countenance my mistress!

GRU. Why, she hath a face of her own.

CURT. Who knows not that?

GRU. Thou, it seems, that calls for company to coun-
tenance her.   90

CURT. I call them forth to credit her.

GRU. Why, she comes to borrow nothing of them.

Enter four or five serving-men

NATH. Welcome home, Grumio!

PHIL. How now, Grumio!

JOS. What, Grumio!

NICH. Fellow Grumio!

NATH. How now, old lad?

GRU. Welcome, you; — how now, you; — what, you; — fellow, you; — and thus much for greeting. Now, my spruce companions, is all ready, and all things neat?   100

---

86 *countenance*] do grace or honour to. "Credit" (line 91) is used in
much the same sense of "conferring credit on." Both words
move Grumio to the like manner of quibbling. "Countenance"
and "credit" are used in a similar connection in Greene's *Vpstart
Courtier* (Greene's *Works*, ed. Grosart, XI, 230): "What is the
end of service to a man, but to *countenance* himselfe and *credite* his
maister with braue suites?"

NATH. All things is ready. How near is our master?

GRU. E'en at hand, alighted by this; and therefore
be not — Cock's passion, silence! I hear my master.

Enter PETRUCHIO *and* KATHARINA

PET. Where be these knaves? What, no man at
    door
To hold my stirrup nor to take my horse!
Where is Nathaniel, Gregory, Philip?

ALL SERV. Here, here, sir; here, sir.

PET. Here, sir! here, sir! here, sir! here sir!
You logger-headed and unpolish'd grooms!
What, no attendance? no regard? no duty?   110
Where is the foolish knave I sent before?

GRU. Here, sir; as foolish as I was before.

PET. You peasant swain! you whoreson malt-horse
    drudge!
Did I not bid thee meet me in the park,
And bring along these rascal knaves with thee?

GRU. Nathaniel's coat, sir, was not fully made,
And Gabriel's pumps were all unpink'd i' the heel;
There was no link to colour Peter's hat,
And Walter's dagger was not come from sheathing:
There were none fine but Adam, Ralph, and Gregory; 120

---

118 *link . . . hat*] Old hats were often blacked over with lampblack
from a torch to give them an appearance of being new. Cf.
Mihil Mumchance (1595?), a tract, wrongly attributed to Robert
Greene, Sig. D. 2: "This cozenage is used likewise in selling old
hats found upon dung-hills, — instead of newe, *blackt over with the
smoake of an old linke.*"

The rest were ragged, old, and beggarly ;
Yet, as they are, here are they come to meet you.
  PET. Go, rascals, go, and fetch my supper in.

                                     [Exeunt servants.

  [*Singing*] Where is the life that late I led —

Where are those — Sit down, Kate, and welcome. —
Soud, soud, soud, soud !

Re-enter Servants *with supper*

Why, when, I say ?   Nay, good sweet Kate, be merry.
Off with my boots, you rogues ! you villains, when ?

  [*Sings*] It was the friar of orders grey,
          As he forth walked on his way :—   130

Out, you rogue ! you pluck my foot awry :
Take that, and mend the plucking off the other.

                                  [Strikes him.

Be merry, Kate.   Some water, here ; what, ho !
Where 's my spaniel Troilus ?   Sirrah, get you hence,

---

124 *Where is the life, etc.*] The same song is quoted by Pistol, *2 Hen. IV*,
    V, iii, 139. The full text has not been discovered. Mention
    is made of it in the heading of a song in Clement Robinson's
    A Handefull of Pleasant Delites (1584) ed. Arber, p. 14 : "Dame
    Beauties replie to the Louer late at libertie : and now complaineth
    himselfe to be her captiue, Intituled : *Where is the life that late I
    led.*" Robinson's song forms a reply to the old ballad.
126 *Soud . . . soud*] An ejaculation expressive of fatigue.
129 *It was a friar of orders grey, etc.*] This is the sole fragment of the
    old ballad which has been preserved. Bishop Percy, in his
    Reliques of Ancient Poetry, developed these two lines into a long
    original poem. The well-known song, beginning " I am a friar of
    orders grey," is a modern composition by John Wall Callcott.

And bid my cousin Ferdinand come hither:
One, Kate, that you must kiss, and be acquainted with.
Where are my slippers? Shall I have some water?

Enter one with water

Come, Kate, and wash, and welcome heartily.
You whoreson villain! will you let it fall? [*Strikes him.*
  KATH. Patience, I pray you; 't was a fault unwilling.
  PET. A whoreson beetle-headed, flap-ear'd knave! 141
Come, Kate, sit down; I know you have a stomach.
Will you give thanks, sweet Kate; or else shall I?
What 's this? mutton?
  FIRST SERV.   Ay.
  PET.   Who brought it?
  PETER.   I.
  PET. 'T is burnt; and so is all the meat.
What dogs are these! where is the rascal cook?
How durst you, villains, bring it from the dresser,
And serve it thus to me that love it not?
There, take it to you, trenchers, cups, and all:
                [*Throws the meat, &c. about the stage.*
You heedless joltheads and unmanner'd slaves! 150
What, do you grumble? I 'll be with you straight.
  KATH. I pray you, husband, be not so disquiet:
The meat was well, if you were so contented.
  PET. I tell thee, Kate, 't was burnt and dried away;
And I expressly am forbid to touch it,

---

135 *cousin Ferdinand*] There is no other mention in the play of this
  personage.

For it engenders choler, planteth anger;
And better 't were that both of us did fast,
Since, of ourselves, ourselves are choleric,
Than feed it with such over-roasted flesh.
Be patient; to-morrow 't shall be mended,   160
And, for this night, we 'll fast for company:
Come, I will bring thee to thy bridal chamber. [*Exeunt.*

Re-enter Servants *severally*

NATH. Peter, didst ever see the like?
PETER. He kills her in her own humour.

Re-enter CURTIS

GRU. Where is he?
CURT. In her chamber, making a sermon of conti-
        nency to her;
And rails, and swears, and rates, that she, poor soul,
Knows not which way to stand, to look, to speak,
And sits as one new-risen from a dream.   170
Away, away! for he is coming hither. [*Exeunt.*

Re-enter PETRUCHIO

PET. Thus have I politicly begun my reign,
And 't is my hope to end successfully.
My falcon now is sharp and passing empty;

---

158 *choleric*] Cf. *Com. of Errors*, II, ii, 61.
174 *seq.*] This and the next six lines develop imagery derived from
    the sport of falconry. The full-fed hawk or falcon is not deceived
    by the "lure" or decoy made to look like a pigeon. A better
    way to master the "haggard" or wild falcon is to keep it awake

And till she stoop she must not be full-gorged,
For then she never looks upon her lure.
Another way I have to man my haggard,
To make her come and know her keeper's call,
That is, to watch her, as we watch these kites
That bate and beat and will not be obedient.   180
She eat no meat to-day, nor none shall eat;
Last night she slept not, nor to-night she shall not;
As with the meat, some undeserved fault
I 'll find about the making of the bed;
And here I 'll fling the pillow, there the bolster,
This way the coverlet, another way the sheets:
Ay, and amid this hurly I intend
That all is done in reverend care of her;
And in conclusion she shall watch all night:
And if she chance to nod, I 'll rail and brawl,   190
And with the clamour keep her still awake.
This is a way to kill a wife with kindness;
And thus I 'll curb her mad and headstrong humour.
He that knows better how to tame a shrew,
Now let him speak: 't is charity to show.   [*Exit.*

---

or watchful, as is done with unruly kites that bate or flutter about
and will not obey the falconer's call.

187 *intend*] pretend; a common usage. Cf. *Much Ado*, II, ii, 32:
"*Intend* a kind of zeal."

192 *kill . . . kindness*] a proverbial expression, which at a later date
suggested to Thomas Heywood the title of his play, *A Woman
killed with Kindness* (1607).

194 *shrew*] This word here rhymes with "show," and thereby illus-
trates the contemporary pronunciation. See note on *L. L. L.*,
V, ii, 46, and cf. *infra*, V, ii, 28 and 188.

SCENE II — PADUA

BEFORE BAPTISTA'S HOUSE

Enter TRANIO *and* HORTENSIO

TRA. Is 't possible, friend Licio, that Mistress Bianca
Doth fancy any other but Lucentio?
I tell you, sir, she bears me fair in hand.
HOR. Sir, to satisfy you in what I have said,
Stand by and mark the manner of his teaching.

Enter BIANCA *and* LUCENTIO

LUC. Now, mistress, profit you in what you read?
BIAN. What, master, read you? first resolve me that.
LUC. I read that I profess, the Art to Love.
BIAN. And may you prove, sir, master of your art!
LUC. While you, sweet dear, prove mistress of my
        heart!   10
HOR. Quick proceeders, marry! Now, tell me, I pray,
You that durst swear that your mistress Bianca
Loved none in the world so well as Lucentio.
TRA. O despiteful love! unconstant womankind!
I tell thee, Licio, this is wonderful.
HOR. Mistake no more: I am not Licio,
Nor a musician, as I seem to be;
But one that scorn to live in this disguise,
For such a one as leaves a gentleman,
And makes a god of such a cullion: 20
Know, sir, that I am call'd Hortensio.

---

20 *cullion*] Cf. Florio's *Italian-English Dictionary*, "coglione a *cuglion*, a .
    gull, a meacoke."

TRA. Signior Hortensio, I have often heard
Of your entire affection to Bianca;
And since mine eyes are witness of her lightness,
I will with you, if you be so contented,
Forswear Bianca and her love for ever.

HOR. See, how they kiss and court! Signior Lucentio,
Here is my hand, and here I firmly vow
Never to woo her more, but do forswear her,
As one unworthy all the former favours   30
That I have fondly flatter'd her withal.

TRA. And here I take the like unfeigned oath,
Never to marry with her though she would entreat:
Fie on her! see, how beastly she doth court him!

HOR. Would all the world but he had quite for-
            sworn!
For me, that I may surely keep mine oath,
I will be married to a wealthy widow,
Ere three days pass, which hath as long loved me
As I have loved this proud disdainful haggard.
And so farewell, Signior Lucentio.   40
Kindness in women, not their beauteous looks,
Shall win my love: and so I take my leave,
In resolution as I swore before.   [Exit.

TRA. Mistress Bianca, bless you with such grace
As 'longeth to a lover's blessed case!
Nay, I have ta'en you napping, gentle love,
And have forsworn you with Hortensio.

BIAN. Tranio, you jest: but have you both forsworn
            me?

TRA. Mistress, we have.

[86]

Luc.   Then we are rid of Licio.
TRA. I' faith, he 'll have a lusty widow now,   50
That shall be woo'd and wedded in a day.
BIAN. God give him joy!
TRA. Ay, and he 'll tame her.
BIAN.   He says so, Tranio.
TRA. Faith, he is gone unto the taming-school.
BIAN. The taming-school! what, is there such a place?
TRA. Ay, mistress, and Petruchio is the master;
That teacheth tricks eleven and twenty long,
To tame a shrew and charm her chattering tongue.

Enter BIONDELLO

BION. O master, master, I have watch'd so long
That I am dog-weary! but at last I spied   60
An ancient angel coming down the hill,
Will serve the turn.
TRA.   What is he, Biondello?
BION. Master, a mercatante, or a pedant,

---

54 *Faith, etc.*] This and the next two lines are borrowed almost verbatim
   from the old play *The Taming of A Shrew.*
57 *tricks eleven and twenty long*] tricks of great intricacy or efficacy.
   There may be some reference to the game of cards, known as
   "one-and-thirty" (eleven *plus* twenty), or "bone-ace," to which
   Grumio has already alluded, I, ii, 32, *supra.*
61 *ancient angel*] Cf. Cotgrave, *Fr.-Engl. Dict.*, "Angelot à la grosse
   escaille: an old angel, and by Metaphor a fellow of the old, sound,
   honest and worthie stamp."
63 *mercatante*] Cf. Florio's *Italian-English Dict.*, "Mercaténte, a Mar-
   chant, a Marter, a Trader."

[87]

I know not what; but formal in apparel,
In gait and countenance surely like a father.

   LUC. And what of him, Tranio?

   TRA. If he be credulous and trust my tale,
I 'll make him glad to seem Vincentio,
And give assurance to Baptista Minola,
As if he were the right Vincentio.   70
Take in your love, and then let me alone.

            [*Exeunt Lucentio and Bianca.*

Enter a Pedant

   PED. God save you, sir!

   TRA.   And you, sir! you are welcome.
Travel you far on, or are you at the farthest?

   PED. Sir, at the farthest for a week or two:
But then up farther, and as far as Rome;
And so to Tripoli, if God lend me life.

   TRA. What countryman, I pray?

   PED.   Of Mantua.

   TRA. Of Mantua, sir? marry, God forbid! ;
And come to Padua, careless of your life?

   PED. My life, sir! how, I pray? for that goes hard.   80

   TRA. 'T is death for any one in Mantua
To come to Padua. Know you not the cause?
Your ships are stay'd at Venice; and the Duke,
For private quarrel 'twixt your duke and him,
Hath publish'd and proclaim'd it openly:

---

81 *'T is death . . . Mantua*] This looks like a reminiscence of *Com. of Errors*, I, i, 19–20: "If any Syracusian born Come to the bay of Ephesus, he dies."

'T is marvel, but that you are but newly come,
You might have heard it else proclaim'd about.

PED. Alas, sir, it is worse for me than so!
For I have bills for money by exchange
From Florence, and must here deliver them. 90

TRA. Well, sir, to do you courtesy,
This will I do, and this I will advise you:
First, tell me, have you ever been at Pisa?

PED. Ay, sir, in Pisa have I often been;
Pisa renowned for grave citizens.

TRA. Among them know you one Vincentio?

PED. I know him not, but I have heard of him;
A merchant of incomparable wealth.

TRA. He is my father, sir; and, sooth to say,
In countenance somewhat doth resemble you. 100

BION. As much as an apple doth an oyster, and all
            one.   [Aside.

TRA. To save your life in this extremity,
This favour will I do you for his sake;
And think it not the worst of all your fortunes
That you are like to Sir Vincentio.
His name and credit shall you undertake,
And in my house you shall be friendly lodged:
Look that you take upon you as you should;
You understand me, sir: so shall you stay
Till you have done your business in the city: 110
If this be courtesy, sir, accept of it.

---

95 *Pisa . . . citizens*] This line has already appeared, I, i, 10, *supra*.
101 *apple . . . oyster*] a proverbial expression implying total want of
    similarity.

[89]

PED. O sir, I do; and will repute you ever
The patron of my life and liberty.
    TRA. Then go with me to make the matter good.
This, by the way, I let you understand;
My father is here look'd for every day,
To pass assurance of a dower in marriage
'Twixt me and one Baptista's daughter here:
In all these circumstances I 'll instruct you:
Go with me to clothe you as becomes you.   [*Exeunt.* 190

SCENE III — A ROOM IN PETRUCHIO'S HOUSE

Enter KATHARINA *and* GRUMIO

GRU. No, no, forsooth; I dare not for my life.
    KATH. The more my wrong, the more his spite
        appears:
What, did he marry me to famish me?
Beggars, that come unto my father's door,
Upon entreaty have a present alms;
If not, elsewhere they meet with charity:
But I, who never knew how to entreat,
Nor never needed that I should entreat,
Am starved for meat, giddy for lack of sleep;
With oaths kept waking, and with brawling fed: 10
And that which spites me more than all these wants,
He does it under name of perfect love;
As who should say, if I should sleep or eat,

---

117 *To pass assurance*] To make settlement.   Cf. *infra*, IV, iv, 45 and 89.

'T were deadly sickness or else present death.
I prithee go and get me some repast ;
I care not what, so it be wholesome food.

  GRU. What say you to a neat's foot ?

  KATH. 'T is passing good : I prithee let me have it.

  GRU. I fear it is too choleric a meat.

How say you to a fat tripe finely broil'd ?   20

  KATH. I like it well : good Grumio, fetch it me.

  GRU. I cannot tell ; I fear 't is choleric.

What say you to a piece of beef and mustard ?

  KATH. A dish that I do love to feed upon.

  GRU. Ay, but the mustard is too hot a little.

  KATH. Why then, the beef, and let the mustard rest.

  GRU. Nay then, I will not : you shall have the mus-
          tard,

Or else you get no beef of Grumio.

  KATH. Then both, or one, or any thing thou wilt.

  GRU. Why then, the mustard without the beef.   30

  KATH. Go, get thee gone, thou false deluding slave,

                            [Beats him.

That feed'st me with the very name of meat :
Sorrow on thee and all the pack of you
That triumph thus upon my misery !
Go, get thee gone, I say.

       Enter PETRUCHIO *and* HORTENSIO *with meat*

  PET. How fares my Kate ? What, sweeting, all
      amort ?

---

36 *all amort*] downcast, dispirited. Shakespeare only uses the expression once again, *1 Hen. VI*, III, ii, 124. The word is a corruption

Hor. Mistress, what cheer?

Kath.   Faith, as cold as can be.

Pet. Pluck up thy spirits; look cheerfully upon me.
Here, love; thou see'st how diligent I am
To dress thy meat myself and bring it thee: 40
I am sure, sweet Kate, this kindness merits thanks.
What, not a word? Nay, then thou lovest it not;
And all my pains is sorted to no proof.
Here, take away this dish.

Kath.   I pray you, let it stand.

Pet. The poorest service is repaid with thanks;
And so shall mine, before you touch the meat.

Kath. I thank you, sir.

Hor. Signior Petruchio, fie! you are to blame.
Come, Mistress Kate, I'll bear you company.

Pet. Eat it up all, Hortensio, if thou lovest me. [Aside.
Much good do it unto thy gentle heart!   51
Kate, eat apace: and now, my honey love,
Will we return unto thy father's house,
And revel it as bravely as the best,
With silken coats and caps and golden rings,
With ruffs and cuffs and fardingales and things;
With scarfs and fans and double change of bravery,
With amber bracelets, beads and all this knavery.

---

of the French "à la mort," which is also found in the Anglicised
form "alamort;" cf. Fanshawe's Lusiad, V, 85, "to cheer the
alamort."

43 *all . . . proof*] all my labour is to no purpose, has proved of no
value. "Proof" here is used for "approof," i. e. "value."

What, hast thou dined ? The tailor stays thy leisure,
To deck thy body with his ruffling treasure.   60

Enter Tailor

Come, tailor, let us see these ornaments ;
Lay forth the gown.

Enter Haberdasher

What news with you, sir ?
HAB. Here is the cap your worship did bespeak.
PET. Why, this was moulded on a porringer ;
A velvet dish : fie, fie ! 't is lewd and filthy :
Why, 't is a cockle or a walnut-shell,
A knack, a toy, a trick, a baby's cap :
Away with it ! come, let me have a bigger.
KATH. I 'll have no bigger : this doth fit the time,
And gentlewomen wear such caps as these.   70
PET. When you are gentle, you shall have one too,
And not till then.
HOR.   That will not be in haste.   [*Aside.*
KATH. Why, sir, I trust I may have leave to speak ;
And speak I will ; I am no child, no babe :
Your betters have endured me say my mind,
And if you cannot, best you stop your ears.
My tongue will tell the anger of my heart,

---

60 *ruffling treasure*] flaunting finery.
64 *moulded . . . porringer*] In *Hen. VIII*, V, iv, 46, a haberdasher's
wife is derisively credited with wearing on her head a "pinked
porringer," *i. e.* a hat fashioned like a dish with a fluted border.

[93]

Or else my heart concealing it will break;
And rather than it shall, I will be free
Even to the uttermost, as I please, in words.   80

PET. Why, thou say'st true; it is a paltry cap,
A custard-coffin, a bauble, a silken pie:
I love thee well, in that thou likest it not.

KATH. Love me or love me not, I like the cap;
And it I will have, or I will have none.

[Exit Haberdasher.

PET. Thy gown? why, ay: come, tailor, let us see 't.
O mercy, God! what masquing stuff is here?
What 's this? a sleeve? 't is like a demi-cannon:
What, up and down, carved like an apple-tart?
Here 's snip and nip and cut and slish and slash,   90
Like to a censer in a barber's shop:
Why, what, i' devil's name, tailor, call'st thou this?

HOR. I see she 's like to have neither cap nor gown.

[Aside.

TAI. You bid me make it orderly and well,
According to the fashion and the time.

PET. Marry, and did; but if you be remember'd,
I did not bid you mar it to the time.

---

82 *custard-coffin*] "Coffin" was the usual term for the paste covering a "custard," a word usually then applied to the contents of a meat or fruit pie. Cf. *Tit. Andr.*, V, ii, 189: "And of the paste a *coffin* I will make."

87 *masquing stuff*] dress fitted for a masquerade.

88 *demi-cannon*] a large gun, of about six and one-half inches' bore.

91 *censer*] A brazier or fire-pan, in which sweet herbs were kept burning in a barber's shop. The cover was liberally perforated.

Go, hop me over every kennel home,
For you shall hop without my custom, sir:
I 'll none of it: hence! make your best of it.   100
    KATH. I never saw a better-fashion'd gown,
More quaint, more pleasing, nor more commendable:
Belike you mean to make a puppet of me.
    PET. Why, true; he means to make a puppet of thee.
    TAI. She says your worship means to make a puppet
            of her.
    PET. O monstrous arrogance! Thou liest, thou
thread, thou thimble,
Thou yard, three-quarters, half-yard, quarter, nail!
Thou flea, thou nit, thou winter-cricket thou!
Braved in mine own house with a skein of thread?   110
Away, thou rag, thou quantity, thou remnant;
Or I shall so be-mete thee with thy yard,
As thou shalt think on prating whilst thou livest!
I tell thee, I, that thou hast marr'd her gown.
    TAI. Your worship is deceived; the gown is made
Just as my master had direction:
Grumio gave order how it should be done.
    GRU. I gave him no order; I gave him the stuff.
    TAI. But how did you desire it should be made?
    GRU. Marry, sir, with needle and thread.   120
    TAI. But did you not request to have it cut?
    GRU. Thou hast faced many things.
    TAI. I have.

---

122 *faced*] trimmed with facings; with the quibbling implication of
    " confronted impudently " or " defied."

GRU. Face not me: thou hast braved many men; brave not me; I will neither be faced nor braved. I say unto thee, I bid thy master cut out the gown; but I did not bid him cut it to pieces: ergo, thou liest.

TAI. Why, here is the note of the fashion to testify.

PET. Read it.

GRU. The note lies in 's throat, if he say I said so. 130

TAI. [*reads*] " Imprimis, a loose-bodied gown :"

GRU. Master, if ever I said loose-bodied gown, sew me in the skirts of it, and beat me to death with a bottom of brown thread: I said a gown.

PET. Proceed.

TAI. [*reads*] " With a small compassed cape :"

GRU. I confess the cape.

TAI. [*reads*] " With a trunk sleeve :"

GRU. I confess two sleeves.

TAI. [*reads*] " The sleeves curiously cut." 140

PET. Ay, there 's the villany.

GRU. Error i' the bill, sir; error i' the bill. I commanded the sleeves should be cut out, and sewed up again; and that I 'll prove upon thee, though thy little finger be armed in a thimble.

TAI. This is true that I say: an I had thee in place where, thou shouldst know it.

GRU. I am for thee straight: take thou the bill, give me thy mete-yard, and spare not me.

---

136 *compassed*] circular. Cf. *Troil. and Cress.*, I, ii, 106 : " the compassed window," *i. e.* circular, bow window.

148 *take . . . bill*] a quibble on the two senses of the word, *i. e.* a tradesman's account and a foot-soldier's weapon.

HOR. God-a-mercy, Grumio! then he shall have no
odds.   150

PET. Well, sir, in brief, the gown is not for me.

GRU. You are i' the right, sir: 't is for my mistress.

PET. Go, take it up unto thy master's use.

GRU. Villain, not for thy life: take up my mistress'
gown for thy master's use!

PET. Why, sir, what 's your conceit in that?

GRU. O, sir, the conceit is deeper than you think for:
Take up my mistress' gown to his master's use!
O, fie, fie, fie!

PET. Hortensio, say thou wilt see the tailor paid.   160
                                                                    [Aside.

Go take it hence; be gone, and say no more.

HOR. Tailor, I 'll pay thee for thy gown to-morrow:
Take no unkindness of his hasty words:
Away! I say; commend me to thy master. [Exit Tailor.

PET. Well, come, my Kate; we will unto your
                father's
Even in these honest mean habiliments:
Our purses shall be proud, our garments poor;
For 't is the mind that makes the body rich;
And as the sun breaks through the darkest clouds,
So honour peereth in the meanest habit.   170
What is the jay more precious than the lark,
Because his feathers are more beautiful?
Or is the adder better than the eel,
Because his painted skin contents the eye?

---

170 *peereth*] appeareth.

O, no, good Kate; neither art thou the worse
For this poor furniture and mean array.
If thou account'st it shame, lay it on me;
And therefore frolic: we will hence forthwith,
To feast and sport us at thy father's house.
Go, call my men, and let us straight to him;   180
And bring our horses unto Long-lane end;
There will we mount, and thither walk on foot.
Let's see; I think 't is now some seven o'clock,
And well we may come there by dinner-time.

    KATH. I dare assure you, sir, 't is almost two;
And 't will be supper-time ere you come there.

    PET. It shall be seven ere I go to horse:
Look, what I speak, or do, or think to do,
You are still crossing it. Sirs, let 't alone:
I will not go to-day; and ere I do,   190
It shall be what o'clock I say it is.

    HOR. Why, so this gallant will command the sun.

                                  [Exeunt.

SCENE IV — PADUA

BEFORE BAPTISTA'S HOUSE

Enter TRANIO, *and the* Pedant *dressed like* VINCENTIO

    TRA. Sir, this is the house: please it you that I call?

    PED. Ay, what else? and but I be deceived

---

181 *Long-lane end*] a reference to the still existing London thorough-
    fare of Long Lane running from Smithfield to Aldersgate Street.
2 *Ay, what else? . . . deceived*] Why, certainly! and unless I am
    deceived.

Signior Baptista may remember me,
Near twenty years ago, in Genoa,
Where we were lodgers at the Pegasus.

TRA. 'T is well; and hold your own, in any case,
With such austerity as 'longeth to a father.

PED. I warrant you.

Enter BIONDELLO

But, sir, here comes your boy;
'T were good he were school'd.

TRA. Fear you not him.   Sirrah Biondello,   10
Now do your duty throughly, I advise you:
Imagine 't were the right Vincentio.

BION. Tut, fear not me.

TRA. But hast thou done thy errand to Baptista?

BION. I told him that your father was at Venice;
And that you look'd for him this day in Padua.

TRA. Thou 'rt a tall fellow: hold thee that to drink.
Here comes Baptista: set your countenance, sir.

Enter BAPTISTA *and* LUCENTIO

Signior Baptista, you are happily met.
[*To the Pedant*] Sir, this is the gentleman I told you of: 20
I pray you, stand good father to me now,
Give me Bianca for my patrimony.

PED. Soft, son!

---

5 *Pegasus*] There was an inn bearing the sign of the Pegasus in Cheapside.   Cf. *The Returne from Parnassus* (1606): " Meet me an hour
hence at the sign of *the Pegasus* in Cheapside."

Sir, by your leave : having come to Padua
To gather in some debts, my son Lucentio
Made me acquainted with a weighty cause
Of love between your daughter and himself :
And, for the good report I hear of you,
And for the love he beareth to your daughter,
And she to him, to stay him not too long,   30
I am content, in a good father's care,
To have him match'd ; and, if you please to like
No worse than I, upon some agreement
Me shall you find ready and willing
With one consent to have her so bestow'd ;
For curious I cannot be with you,
Signior Baptista, of whom I hear so well.

    BAP. Sir, pardon me in what I have to say :
Your plainness and your shortness please me well.
Right true it is, your son Lucentio here   40
Doth love my daughter, and she loveth him,
Or both dissemble deeply their affections :
And therefore, if you say no more than this,
That like a father you will deal with him,
And pass my daughter a sufficient dower,
The match is made, and all is done :
Your son shall have my daughter with consent.

    TRA. I thank you, sir. Where then do you know best
We be affied and such assurance ta'en
As shall with either part's agreement stand ?   50

---

45 *pass*] make conveyance. Cf. *supra*, IV, ii, 117, and *infra*, 89.
    "Pass" is again used in the somewhat less technical sense of
    "transact," *infra*, line 57 : "We'll *pass* the business."

BAP. Not in my house, Lucentio ; for, you know,
Pitchers have ears, and I have many servants :
Besides, old Gremio is hearkening still ;
And happily we might be interrupted.

TRA. Then at my lodging, an it like you :
There doth my father lie ; and there, this night,
We 'll pass the business privately and well.
Send for your daughter by your servant here ;
My boy shall fetch the scrivener presently.
The worst is this, that, at so slender warning,   60
You are like to have a thin and slender pittance.

BAP. It likes me well. Cambio, hie you home,
And bid Bianca make her ready straight ;
And, if you will, tell what hath happened,
Lucentio's father is arrived in Padua,
And how she 's like to be Lucentio's wife.

BION. I pray the gods she may with all my heart !

TRA. Dally not with the gods, but get thee gone.
[Exit Bion.

Signior Baptista, shall I lead the way ?
Welcome ! one mess is like to be your cheer :   70
Come, sir ; we will better it in Pisa.

BAP. I follow you.
[Exeunt Tranio, Pedant, and Baptista.

Re-enter BIONDELLO

BION. Cambio.

LUC. What sayest thou, Biondello ?

BION. You saw my master wink and laugh upon you ?

LUC. Biondello, what of that ?

[101]

BION. Faith, nothing; but has left me here behind, to expound the meaning or moral of his signs and tokens.

LUC. I pray thee, moralize them.

BION. Then thus. Baptista is safe, talking with the so deceiving father of a deceitful son.

LUC. And what of him?

BION. His daughter is to be brought by you to the supper.

LUC. And then?

BION. The old priest at Saint Luke's church is at your command at all hours.

LUC. And what of all this?

BION. I cannot tell; expect they are busied about a counterfeit assurance: take you assurance of her, "cum privilegio ad imprimendum solum:" to the church; take so the priest, clerk, and some sufficient honest witnesses:
If this be not that you look for, I have no more to say,
But bid Bianca farewell for ever and a day.

LUC. Hearest thou, Biondello?

BION. I cannot tarry: I knew a wench married in an afternoon as she went to the garden for parsley to stuff a rabbit; and so may you, sir: and so, adieu, sir. My master hath appointed me to go to Saint Luke's, to bid the priest be ready to come against you come with your appendix. [*Exit.*

LUC. I may, and will, if she be so contented: 100

---

89 *assurance*] See note on IV, ii, 117, *supra.*
90 *cum privilegio, etc.*] These words were usually inserted in books of which printers had secured, under letters patent, sole copyright.

She will be pleased ; then wherefore should I doubt ?
Hap what hap may, I 'll roundly go about her :
It shall go hard if Cambio go without her.   [*Exit.*

SCENE V — A PUBLIC ROAD

Enter PETRUCHIO, KATHARINA, HORTENSIO *and* Servants

PET. Come on, i' God's name ; once more toward our
    father's.
Good Lord, how bright and goodly shines the moon !
  KATH. The moon ! the sun : it is not moonlight now.
  PET. I say it is the moon that shines so bright.
  KATH. I know it is the sun that shines so bright.
  PET. Now, by my mother's son, and that 's myself,
It shall be moon, or star, or what I list,
Or ere I journey to your father's house.
Go on, and fetch our horses back again.
Evermore cross'd and cross'd ; nothing but cross'd !   10
  HOR. Say as he says, or we shall never go.
  KATH. Forward, I pray, since we have come so far,
And be it moon, or sun, or what you please :
An if you please to call it a rush-candle,
Henceforth I vow it shall be so for me.
  PET. I say it is the moon.
  KATH.   I know it is the moon.
  PET. Nay, then you lie : it is the blessed sun.

---

102 *I 'll roundly . . . her*] I 'll be blunt or outspoken with her. See
    note on I, ii, 57, *supra.*

KATH. Then, God be bless'd, it is the blessed sun :
But sun it is not, when you say it is not ;
And the moon changes even as your mind. 20
What you will have it named, even that it is ;
And so it shall be so for Katharine.
    HOR. Petruchio, go thy ways ; the field is won.
    PET. Well, forward, forward ! thus the bowl should
        run,
And not unluckily against the bias.
But, soft ! company is coming here.

Enter VINCENTIO

[*To Vincentio*] Good morrow, gentle mistress: where
    away ?
Tell me, sweet Kate, and tell me truly too,
Hast thou beheld a fresher gentlewoman ?
Such war of white and red within her cheeks ! 30
What stars do spangle heaven with such beauty,
As those two eyes become that heavenly face ?
Fair lovely maid, once more good day to thee.
Sweet Kate, embrace her for her beauty's sake.

---

25 *against the bias*] contrary to tendency or propensity, a technical
    term in the game of bowls. Cf. *Rich. II*, III, iv, 5: " My
    fortune runs *against the bias*."
30 *Such . . . cheeks*] Cf. *Lucrece*, 71 : " This silent *war of lilies and of
    roses*."
31–32 *What stars . . . face*] Cf. *Sonnet* cxxxii, 7–9 :

    " Nor that full star that ushers in the even
    Doth half that glory to the sober west,
    As those two mourning eyes become thy face."

HOR. A' will make the man mad, to make a woman
of him.

KATH. Young budding virgin, fair and fresh and
sweet,
Whither away, or where is thy abode?
Happy the parents of so fair a child;
Happier the man, whom favourable stars
Allot thee for his lovely bed-fellow!   40

PET. Why, how now, Kate! I hope thou art not
mad:
This is a man, old, wrinkled, faded, wither'd;
And not a maiden, as thou say'st he is.

KATH. Pardon, old father, my mistaking eyes,
That have been so bedazzled with the sun,
That every thing I look on seemeth green:
Now I perceive thou art a reverend father;
Pardon, I pray thee, for my mad mistaking.

PET. Do, good old grandsire; and withal make known
Which way thou travellest: if along with us,   50
We shall be joyful of thy company.

VIN. Fair sir, and you my merry mistress,
That with your strange encounter much amazed me,
My name is call'd Vincentio; my dwelling Pisa;
And bound I am to Padua; there to visit
.A son of mine, which long I have not seen.

PET. What is his name?

VIN.   Lucentio, gentle sir.

PET. Happily met; the happier for thy son.
And now by law, as well as reverend age,
I may entitle thee my loving father: .60

The sister to my wife, this gentlewoman,
Thy son by this hath married.   Wonder not,
Nor be not grieved : she is of good esteem,
Her dowry wealthy, and of worthy birth ;
Beside, so qualified as may beseem
The spouse of any noble gentleman.
Let me embrace with old Vincentio,
And wander we to see thy honest son,
Who will of thy arrival be full joyous.

VIN. But is this true ? or is it else your pleasure,   70
Like pleasant travellers, to break a jest
Upon the company you overtake ?

HOR. I do assure thee, father, so it is.

PET. Come, go along, and see the truth hereof ;
For our first merriment hath made thee jealous.

[Exeunt all but Hortensio.

HOR. Well, Petruchio, this has put me in heart.
Have to my widow ! and if she be froward,
Then hast thou taught Hortensio to be untoward. *[Exit.*

ACT FIFTH — SCENE I — PADUA
BEFORE LUCENTIO'S HOUSE

GREMIO *discovered.* *Enter behind* BIONDELLO, LUCENTIO, *and* BIANCA

BIONDELLO

OFTLY AND SWIFTLY, sir; for the priest is ready.

LUC. I fly, Biondello: but they may chance to need thee at home; therefore leave us.

BION. Nay, faith, I 'll see the church o' your back; and then come back to my master's as soon as I can.

[*Exeunt Lucentio, Bianca, and Biondello.*

GRE. I marvel Cambio comes not all this while.

Enter PETRUCHIO, KATHARINA, VINCENTIO, GRUMIO, *with* Attendants

PET. Sir, here 's the door, this is Lucentio's house:
My father's bears more toward the market-place;
Thither must I, and here I leave you, sir.

[107]

VIN. You shall not choose but drink before you go : 10
I think I shall command your welcome here,
And, by all likelihood, some cheer is toward.   [*Knocks.*
    GRE. They 're busy within; you were best knock
        louder.

Pedant looks out of the window

PED. What 's he that knocks as he would beat down
the gate ?
    VIN. Is Signior Lucentio within, sir ?
    PED. He 's within, sir, but not to be spoken withal.
    VIN. What if a man bring him a hundred pound or
two, to make merry withal ?
    PED. Keep your hundred pounds to yourself : he shall so
need none, so long as I live.
    PET. Nay, I told you your son was well beloved in
Padua. Do you hear, sir ? — to leave frivolous circumstances, — I pray you, tell Signior Lucentio, that
his father is come from Pisa, and is here at the door to
speak with him.
    PED. Thou liest : his father has come from Padua,
and here looking out at the window.
    VIN. Art thou his father ?
    PED. Ay, sir ; so his mother says, if I may believe
her.
    PET. [*To Vincentio*] Why, how now, gentleman ! why, so
this is flat knavery, to take upon you another man's
name.
    PED. Lay hands on the villain : I believe a' means to
cozen somebody in this city under my countenance.

Re-enter BIONDELLO

BION. I have seen them in the church together: God send 'em good shipping! But who is here? mine old master Vincentio! now we are undone, and brought to nothing.

VIN. [*Seeing Biondello*] Come hither, crack-hemp.

BION. I hope I may choose, sir.

VIN. Come hither, you rogue. What, have you for- 40 got me?

BION. Forgot you! no, sir: I could not forget you, for I never saw you before in all my life.

VIN. What, you notorious villain, didst thou never see thy master's father, Vincentio?

BION. What, my old worshipful old master? yes, marry, sir: see where he looks out of the window.

VIN. Is 't so, indeed?   [*Beats Biondello.*

BION. Help, help, help! here 's a madman will murder me.   [*Exit.* 50

PED. Help, son! help, Signior Baptista!
                              [*Exit from above.*

PET. Prithee, Kate, let 's stand aside, and see the end of this controversy.   [*They retire.*

Re-enter Pedant *below;* TRANIO, BAPTISTA, *and* Servants

TRA. Sir, what are you, that offer to beat my servant?

VIN. What am I, sir! nay, what are you, sir? O immortal gods! O fine villain! A silken doublet! a velvet hose! a scarlet cloak! and a copatain hat! O, I am undone! I am undone! while I play the good husband at home, my son and my servant spend all at the university.

TRA. How now! what's the matter?   60

BAP. What, is the man lunatic?

TRA. Sir, you seem a sober ancient gentleman by your habit, but your words show you a madman. Why, sir, what 'cerns it you if I wear pearl and gold? I thank my good father, I am able to maintain it.

VIN. Thy father! O villain! he is a sail-maker in Bergamo.

BAP. You mistake, sir, you mistake, sir. Pray, what do you think is his name?

VIN. His name! as if I knew not his name: I have 70 brought him up ever since he was three years old, and his name is Tranio.

PED. Away, away, mad ass! his name is Lucentio; and he is mine only son, and heir to the lands of me, Signior Vincentio.

VIN. Lucentio! O, he hath murdered his master! Lay hold on him, I charge you, in the Duke's name. O, my son, my son! Tell me, thou villain, where is my son Lucentio?

TRA. Call forth an officer.   80

---

57 *copatain hat*] a hat with a high crown in the form of a sugar-loaf. The word "copatain" is not met in this form elsewhere. It, seems a variant of "copintank" or "copentank," of unknown derivation," which is found in a like sense in 16th century English.

Enter one with an Officer

Carry this mad knave to the gaol. Father Baptista, I
charge you see that he be forthcoming.

VIN. Carry me to the gaol !

GRE. Stay, officer : he shall not go to prison.

BAP. Talk not, Signior Gremio : I say he shall go to
prison.

GRE. Take heed, Signior Baptista, lest you be cony-
catched in this business : I dare swear this is the right
Vincentio.

PED. Swear, if thou darest.   90

GRE. Nay, I dare not swear it.

TRA. Then thou wert best say that I am not
Lucentio.

GRE. Yes, I know thee to be Signior Lucentio.

BAP. Away with the dotard ! to the gaol with him !

VIN. Thus strangers may be haled and abused :
O monstrous villain !

Re-enter BIONDELLO, *with* LUCENTIO *and* BIANCA

BION. O, we are spoiled ! and — yonder he is : deny
him, forswear him, or else we are all undone.

LUC. Pardon, sweet father.   [*Kneeling.*

VIN.   Lives my sweet son ?
[*Exeunt Biondello, Tranio, and Pedant, as fast as may be.*

BIAN. Pardon, dear father.

BAP.   How hast thou offended ? 100
Where is Lucentio ?

LUC.   Here 's Lucentio,

[111]

Right son to the right Vincentio;
That have by marriage made thy daughter mine,
While counterfeit supposes blear'd thine eyne.

GRE. Here's packing, with a witness, to deceive us
all!

VIN. Where is that damned villain Tranio,
That faced and braved me in this matter so?

BAP. Why, tell me, is not this my Cambio?

BIAN. Cambio is changed into Lucentio.

LUC. Love wrought these miracles. Bianca's love   110
Made me exchange my state with Tranio,
While he did bear my countenance in the town;
And happily I have arrived at the last
Unto the wished haven of my bliss.
What Tranio did, myself enforced him to;
Then pardon him, sweet father, for my sake.

VIN. I'll slit the villain's nose, that would have sent
me to the gaol.

BAP. But do you hear, sir? have you married my
daughter without asking my good will?   120

VIN. Fear not, Baptista; we will content you, go to:
but I will in, to be revenged for this villany.   [Exit.

BAP. And I, to sound the depth of this knavery. [Exit.

---

104 *counterfeit supposes*] false assumptions or suppositions. Florio in his
Italian-Engl. Dict. interprets the Italian noun "supposito" as "a
suppose or thing supposed." George Gascoigne translated Ariosto's
play of *Gli Suppositi* under the name of *The Supposes.*

105 *Here's packing, with a witness*] Here's a gross piece of plotting,
of a surety; here's trickery, beyond all question.

LUC. Look not pale, Bianca; thy father will not
frown.   [*Exeunt Lucentio and Bianca.*

GRE. My cake is dough: but I'll in among the
   rest;

Out of hope of all, but my share of the feast.   [*Exit.*

KATH. Husband, let's follow, to see the end of this
ado.

PET. First kiss me, Kate, and we will.

KATH. What, in the midst of the street?

PET. What, art thou ashamed of me?   130

KATH. No, sir, God forbid; but ashamed to kiss.

PET. Why, then let's home again. Come, sirrah,
   let's away.

KATH. Nay, I will give thee a kiss: now pray thee,
   love, stay.

PET. Is not this well? Come, my sweet Kate:
Better once than never, for never too late.   [*Exeunt.*

SCENE II — PADUA

LUCENTIO'S HOUSE

Enter BAPTISTA, VINCENTIO, GREMIO, *the* Pedant, LUCENTIO, BIANCA,
PETRUCHIO, KATHARINA, HORTENSIO, *and* Widow, TRANIO, BION-
DELLO, *and* GRUMIO: *the Serving-men with Tranio bringing in a
banquet.*

LUC. At last, though long, our jarring notes agree:
And time it is, when raging war is done,

---

125 *My cake is dough*] It's all up with me. This proverbial expression
 of discomfiture has already figured, I, i, 108, *supra.*

To smile at scapes and perils overblown.
My fair Bianca, bid my father welcome,
While I with self-same kindness welcome thine.
Brother Petruchio, sister Katharina,
And thou, Hortensio, with thy loving widow,
Feast with the best, and welcome to my house:
My banquet is to close our stomachs up,
After our great good cheer.   Pray you, sit down;   10
For now we sit to chat, as well as eat.

PET. Nothing but sit and sit, and eat and eat!
BAP. Padua affords this kindness, son Petruchio.
PET. Padua affords nothing but what is kind.
HOR. For both our sakes, I would that word were
　　　true.
PET. Now, for my life, Hortensio fears his widow.
WID. Then never trust me, if I be afeard.
PET. You are very sensible, and yet you miss my
　　　sense:
I mean, Hortensio is afeard of you.
WID. He that is giddy thinks the world turns round. 20
PET. Roundly replied.
KATH.　　　　　Mistress, how mean you that?

---

9 *banquet*] In Shakespeare's day this word was largely restricted to
after-dinner dessert or a slight repast between meals. Cf. "a
running *banquet*" (*i. e.* a hasty refreshment), *Hen. VIII*, I, iv, 12.
The word was not wholly confined to the sense of a sumptuous
feast till the 18th century.

16–17 *fears . . . afeard*] The widow understands Petruchio to use the
word "fears" in the causative sense of "frightens," instead of in
the normal passive sense of "dread."

WID. Thus I conceive by him.

PET. Conceives by me! How likes Hortensio that?

HOR. My widow says, thus she conceives her tale.

PET. Very well mended. Kiss him for that, good
    widow.

KATH. "He that is giddy thinks the world turns
    round:"

I pray you, tell me what you meant by that.

WID. Your husband, being troubled with a shrew,

Measures my husband's sorrow by his woe:

And now you know my meaning.   30

KATH. A very mean meaning.

WID.   Right, I mean you.

KATH. And I am mean, indeed, respecting you.

PET. To her, Kate!

HOR. To her, widow!

PET. A hundred marks, my Kate does put her down.

HOR. That's my office.

PET. Spoke like an officer: ha' to thee, lad.

                [*Drinks to Hortensio.*

BAP. How likes Gremio these quick-witted folks?

GRE. Believe me, sir, they butt together well.

BIAN. Head, and butt! an hasty-witted body   40

Would say your head and butt were head and horn.

VIN. Ay, mistress bride, hath that awaken'd you?

BIAN. Ay, but not frighted me; therefore I'll sleep
    again.

---

28 *shrew*] "shrew" here rhymes with "woe." See note on IV, i, 194,
  supra, and 188, *infra.*

PET. Nay, that you shall not : since you have begun,
Have at you for a bitter jest or two !

BIAN. Am I your bird ? I mean to shift my bush ;
And then pursue me as you draw your bow.
You are welcome all. [*Exeunt Bianca, Katharina, and Widow.*

PET. She hath prevented me.   Here, Signior Tranio,
This bird you aim'd at, though you hit her not ;   50
Therefore a health to all that shot and miss'd.

TRA. O, sir, Lucentio slipp'd me like his greyhound,
Which runs himself, and catches for his master.

PET. A good swift simile, but something currish.

TRA. 'T is well, sir, that you hunted for yourself :
'T is thought your deer does hold you at a bay.

BAP. O ho, Petruchio ! Tranio hits you now.

LUC. I thank thee for that gird, good Tranio.

HOR. Confess, confess, hath he not hit you here ?

PET. A' has a little gall'd me, I confess ;   60
And, as the jest did glance away from me,
'T is ten to one it maim'd you two outright.

BAP. Now, in good sadness, son Petruchio,
I think thou hast the veriest shrew of all.

PET. Well, I say no : and therefore for assurance
Let 's each one send unto his wife ;
And he whose wife is most obedient,
To come at first when he doth send for her,
Shall win the wager which we will propose.

---

63 *in good sadness*] in sober earnest. The common phrase is met with
in *All's Well*, IV, iii, 230, and twice in *Merry Wives*, III, v, 109, and
IV, ii, 79.

HOR. Content. What is the wager?

LUC.   Twenty crowns. 70

PET. Twenty crowns!

I 'll venture so much of my hawk or hound,

But twenty times so much upon my wife.

LUC. A hundred then.

HOR.   Content.

PET.   A match! 't is done.

HOR. Who shall begin?

LUC.   That will I.

Go, Biondello, bid your mistress come to me.

BION. I go.   [*Exit.*

BAP. Son, I 'll be your half, Bianca comes.

LUC. I 'll have no halves; I 'll bear it all myself.

Re-enter BIONDELLO

How now! what news?

BION.   Sir, my mistress sends you word so

That she is busy, and she cannot come.

PET. How! she is busy, and she cannot come!

Is that an answer?

GRE.   Ay, and a kind one too:

Pray God, sir, your wife send you not a worse.

PET. I hope, better.

HOR. Sirrah Biondello, go and entreat my wife

To come to me forthwith.   [*Exit Biondello.*

PET.   O, ho! entreat her!

Nay, then she must needs come.

HOR.   I am afraid, sir,

Do what you can, yours will not be entreated.

Re-enter BIONDELLO

Now, where's my wife?   90

BION. She says you have some goodly jest in
    hand:
She will not come; she bids you come to her.

PET. Worse and worse; she will not come! O vile,
Intolerable, not to be endured!
Sirrah Grumio, go to your mistress;
Say, I command her come to me.   [*Exit Grumio.*

HOR. I know her answer.

PET.   What?

HOR.   She will not.

PET. The fouler fortune mine, and there an end.

BAP. Now, by my holidame, here comes Katharina!

Re-enter KATHARINA

KATH. What is your will, sir, that you send for me? 100

PET. Where is your sister, and Hortensio's wife?

KATH. They sit conferring by the parlour fire.

PET. Go, fetch them hither: if they deny to come,
Swinge me them soundly forth unto their husbands:
Away, I say, and bring them hither straight.

[*Exit Katharina.*

LUC. Here is a wonder, if you talk of a wonder.

HOR. And so it is: I wonder what it bodes.

PET. Marry, peace it bodes, and love, and quiet
    life,
An awful rule, and right supremacy;
And, to be short, what not, that's sweet and happy? 110

BAP. Now, fair befal thee, good Petruchio!
The wager thou hast won; and I will add
Unto their losses twenty thousand crowns;
Another dowry to another daughter,
For she is changed, as she had never been.
PET. Nay, I will win my wager better yet,
And show more sign of her obedience,
Her new-built virtue and obedience.
See where she comes and brings your froward wives
As prisoners to her womanly persuasion.   190

Re-enter KATHARINA, *with* BIANCA *and* Widow

Katharine, that cap of yours becomes you not:
Off with that bauble, throw it under-foot.
WID. Lord, let me never have a cause to sigh,
Till I be brought to such a silly pass!
BIAN. Fie, what a foolish duty call you this?
LUC. I would your duty were as foolish too:
The wisdom of your duty, fair Bianca,
Hath cost me an hundred crowns since supper-time.
BIAN. The more fool you, for laying on my duty.
PET. Katharine, I charge thee, tell these headstrong
        women   130
What duty they do owe their lords and husbands.
WID. Come, come, you 're mocking: we will have no
        telling.
PET. Come on, I say; and first begin with her.
WID. She shall not.
PET. I say she shall: and first begin with her.

KATH. Fie, fie! unknit that threatening unkind brow;
And dart not scornful glances from those eyes,
To wound thy lord, thy king, thy governor:
It blots thy beauty as frosts do bite the meads,
Confounds thy fame as whirlwinds shake fair buds,   140
And in no sense is meet or amiable.
A woman moved is like a fountain troubled,
Muddy, ill-seeming, thick, bereft of beauty;
And while it is so, none so dry or thirsty
Will deign to sip or touch one drop of it.
Thy husband is thy lord, thy life, thy keeper,
Thy head, thy sovereign; one that cares for thee,
And for thy maintenance commits his body
To painful labour both by sea and land,
To watch the night in storms, the day in cold,   150
Whilst thou liest warm at home, secure and safe;
And craves no other tribute at thy hands
But love, fair looks and true obedience;
Too little payment for so great a debt.
Such duty as the subject owes the prince
Even such a woman oweth to her husband;
And when she is froward, peevish, sullen, sour,
And not obedient to his honest will,
What is she but a foul contending rebel,
And graceless traitor to her loving lord?   160
I am ashamed that women are so simple
To offer war where they should kneel for peace;
Or seek for rule, supremacy and sway,
When they are bound to serve, love and obey.
Why are our bodies soft and weak and smooth,

Unapt to toil and trouble in the world,
But that our soft conditions and our hearts
Should well agree with our external parts?
Come, come, you froward and unable worms!
My mind hath been as big as one of yours,   170
My heart as great, my reason haply more,
To bandy word for word and frown for frown;
But now I see our lances are but straws,
Our strength as weak, our weakness past compare,
That seeming to be most which we indeed least are.
Then vail your stomachs, for it is no boot,
And place your hands below your husband's foot:
In token of which duty, if he please,
My hand is ready, may it do him ease.

    PET. Why, there's a wench! Come on, and kiss me,
      Kate.   180
    LUC. Well, go thy ways, old lad; for thou shalt
      ha't.
    VIN. 'T is a good hearing, when children are toward.
    LUC. But a harsh hearing, when women are froward.
    PET. Come, Kate, we'll to bed.
We three are married, but you two are sped.
'T was I won the wager, though you hit the white;

                                  [*To Lucentio.*

---

167 *soft conditions*] gentle qualities (of mind).
176 *vail your stomachs*] abate your pride. Cf. *2 Hen. IV*, I, i, 129:
    "The bloody Douglas . . . 'Gan *vail* his *stomach*."
    it is no boot] there is no advantage.
185 *you two are sped*] you two are undone, done for.
186 *hit the white*] hit the bull's eye, with a play on Bianca's name,
    which is the Italian word for "white."

And, being a winner, God give you good night!

[Exeunt Petruchio and Katharina.

Hor. Now, go thy ways; thou hast tamed a curst
shrew.

Luc. 'T is a wonder, by your leave, she will be tamed
so. *[Exeunt.*

---

188 *shrew*] pronounced to rhyme with "so." Cf. note on IV, i, 194,
and line 28, *supra.*

THE COMPLETE WORKS OF
WILLIAM SHAKESPEARE

WITH ANNOTATIONS AND
A GENERAL INTRODUCTION
BY SIDNEY LEE

VOLUME IV

THE MERRY WIVES OF WINDSOR

WITH A SPECIAL INTRODUCTION BY AUSTIN DOBSON
AND AN ORIGINAL FRONTISPIECE BY W. H. MARGETSON

CONTENTS

INTRODUCTION

ONCERNING the origin of "The Merry Wives of Windsor," there is — what there is not always in the case of Shakespeare's plays — at least one time-honoured tradition. It is said to have been written by command of Queen Elizabeth. The first mention of this tradition occurs in the "Epistle Dedicatory" of "The Comical Gallant: or the Amours of Sir John Falstaffe," a comedy produced at Drury Lane in 1702 by the clever but cross-grained old critic, John Dennis (Pope's "Appius"), who, in the occultation of Shakespeare at the opening of the eighteenth century, appears to have imagined that he could concoct from "The Merry Wives of Windsor" something better suited to the court of Queen Anne. "The Comical Gallant" had no success, and deserved none. But the "Epistle Dedicatory" contained one memorable utterance. "I knew very well," says Dennis, "that it ["The Merry Wives of Windsor"] had pleas'd one of the greatest Queens that ever was in the World.... This comedy [the "Merry Wives" again] was written at her Command, and by her direction, and she was so eager to see it Acted, that she commanded it to be finished in fourteen days; and was afterwards, as Tradition tells us, very well pleas'd at the Representation." Dennis again refers to the story in the Prologue:—

"But *Shakespear's* Play in fourteen days was writ,
And in that space to make all just and fit,
Was an attempt surpassing human Wit.
Yet our great *Shakespear's* matchless Muse was such,
None e'er in so small time perform'd so much."

As regards the last lines Dennis should have remembered that, sixty years after Shakespeare, Molière had run that "matchless Muse" very close in point of speed. The comedy of "Les Facheux," which was prepared for the fête given by Fouquet to Louis XIV. in 1661, was "*conçue, faite, apprise et représentée en quinze jours.*" But this is by the way. The tradition to which Dennis first gave currency was promptly repeated with additions. In Rowe's "Life of Shakespeare" (Works, 1709, pp. viii–ix) he writes: "She [Queen Elizabeth] was so well pleas'd with that admirable Character of *Falstaff*, in the two Parts of "Henry the Fourth," that she commanded him to continue it for one Play more, and to show him in Love. This is said to be the Occasion of his writing "The Merry Wives of Windsor." How well she was obey'd, the Play it self is an admirable proof." To Rowe in 1710 followed Charles Gildon, who in his "Remarks on the Plays of Shakespear," p. 291, wrote: "The *Fairys* in the fifth Act makes a Handsome complement to the Queen, in her palace of *Windsor*, who had oblig'd him [Shakespeare] to write a Play of Sir *John Falstaff* in Love, and which I am very well assured he perform'd in a Fortnight; a prodigious Thing, when all is so well contriv'd, and carry'd on without the least Confusion." It will be observed that Dennis, writing long after the event, gives no authority beyond the assertion, "I knew very well"; and it is difficult to say whether Rowe and Gildon had other information, or simply embroidered Dennis. But their combined statements have been generally accepted as evidence of a definite tradition, and, as we shall see presently, the "Merry Wives" was played before the Queen, whether written at her command or not.

With regard to the date of the composition of the "Merry Wives," we are, although still in the land of conjecture, upon somewhat surer ground. Falstaff appears in two other plays of Shakespeare, — the First and Second Parts of "Henry IV."; while in Act II., Sc. 3, of "Henry V." Mrs. Quickly narrates his death. The First Part of "Henry IV." is supposed to have been written in 1596–7, the Second Part in 1597–8, and "King Henry V." in 1599. In order to desire to see Falstaff in a new light, Queen Elizabeth must obviously have seen him already upon the stage; and it is probable that she had made acquaintance with him either in the First Part of "Henry IV." or in the Second Part, or in both. If in both, the date of the composition of the "Merry Wives" cannot be placed earlier than 1597; if in the First Part only, then not later than 1596. By general agreement of the commentators, the probable date of composition has been fixed at 1599, the date assigned for the composition of "Henry V.," and it has been further supposed that it was written immediately after that play, or about Christmas. Of course it may have been written later. But the argument that Shakespeare, who, in the person of Justice Shallow, revenges himself upon his old enemy Sir Thomas Lucy of Charlecote, would not have pursued that revenge beyond the grave, is not without its force; and Lucy died in July, 1600. To another speculation, which would have the effect of placing the date of the composition of "The Merry Wives of Windsor" much earlier than even 1596, we need only refer historically, as it has now been practically abandoned. In the year 1592 a visit was paid to Queen Elizabeth at Windsor by a certain Duke of Wurtemberg or Count of Mömpelgard, who, or whose following, is supposed to be glanced at in the account given in the play of fraud practised on Mine Host of the Garter (Act IV., Sc. 5) by German visitors to Windsor; and indeed, in the earlier version of the play, the name of Mömpelgard is held to be specifically indicated in the "cosen garmombles" of Sir Hugh Evans. But apart from the very obvious comment that no allusion to a royal visitor of an offensive nature could have been permitted in a play represented before the court, the effect of this suggestion would be to throw the composition back to a date preceding the dates of the two Parts of " Henry IV.," and so to overturn the whole fabric of the connection of the " Merry Wives " with the desire of Queen Elizabeth to see the Falstaff of those plays " in love." Whether "one of the greatest Queens that ever was in the World " was wise in throwing such a task upon the greatest of the world's dramatists may be questioned ; and in any case, it depends not a little upon the exact interpretation which was attached to being " in love" in the court of " Gloriana," now nearing the end of her career.

But whether " The Merry Wives of Windsor " was written at the end of 1599 or earlier, it was certainly printed in its earliest form in 1602. In the Registers of the Stationers' Company are the following entries :—

" 18 Jan., 1601-2.
" John Busby.] An Excellent and pleasant conceited Commedie of Sir John Faulstof, and the Merrie Wyves of Windesor.
" Arthur Johnson.] By assignment from John Busbye a book. An excellent and pleasant conceited comedie of Sir John Faulstafe and the merry wyves of Windsor."

The title of the play subsequently issued is as follows : " A most pleasaunt and excellent conceited Comedie, of Sir *John Falstaffe*, and the merrie Wiues of *Windsor*. Entermixed with sundrie variable and pleasing humors, of Syr *Hugh*, the Welch Knight, Justice *Shallow*, and his wise Cousin M. *Slender*. With the swaggering vaine of Auncient *Pistoll,* and Corporall *Nym.* By William Shakespeare." Then comes the announcement: "As it hath been diuers times Acted by the right Honorable my Lord Chamberlaine's seruants. Both before her Maiestie and elsewhere. London: Printed by T. C. [i. e. Thomas Creede] for Arthur Johnson, and are to be sold at his shop in Powles Church yard, at the signe of the Flower de Leuse and the Crowne. 1602." A reprint of this quarto was issued in 1619, and a fuller version divided into Acts and Scenes was included in the folio of 1623. Of this fuller version a quarto edition was published in 1630. The exact relation of the quarto version of 1602 to the folio version of 1623 is one of the *cruces* of the commentators. Halliwell, who, in 1842, issued a reprint of the quarto for the Shakespeare Society, both regarded it and described it as a "first sketch," advancing minute arguments to that effect. On the other hand, Mr. P. A. Daniel, who printed a photo-lithographic *facsimile,* does not accept this view. He regards the folio and the quarto as imperfect copies of a common and now non-existent original, — the quarto being a note-taker's version of that original after it had been shortened for stage purposes, and the folio a fuller but still imperfect and unauthentic version of the same. The question is still *sub judice.* Mr. Howard Furness has not yet included the "Merry Wives" in his Variorum Edition; but scholars seem disposed at present to espouse the theory of Mr. Daniel. With regard to the contention that the play, as we have it, is still imperfect, may be mentioned the references (Act III., Scs. 1 and 3, and Act IV., Sc. 5) to some obscure retaliation by Caius and Evans upon the Host of the Garter which appears to be connected with the "cozening Germans" who steal his horses in Act IV. It is scarcely possible that such retaliation should be confined to jeering at him in his misfortune; and it may be that Pistol and Nym, who disappear early in the play (and even their old ally Bardolph, who relates the circumstances of the horse stealing), were not unconnected with it.

Unlike many of Shakespeare's works, the "Merry Wives" seems to owe but little of its plot to previous writers. Obviously time pressed; and Shakespeare was obliged on this occasion to depend more than usual upon the riches of his own imagination. Another reason which threw him upon his personal resources in this particular case would no doubt be that the scene of the play was laid at the date of representation, and his material lay about, and not behind him. But at the end of his edition of the quarto of 1602 Halliwell prints a number of tales, which may conceivably have been more or less remotely in Shakespeare's mind when he devised his incidents. One of these is contained in Ser Giovanni's "Il Pecorone," and of this there is an English version entitled "The Fortunate, the Deceived, and the Unfortunate Lovers," dated 1632. If Shakespeare used this story, he must have of course employed the original Italian or some earlier version; but the husband who figures in it is certainly befooled in the same way as Ford in the play, while the gallant not only communicates his designs to him, but is concealed by the wife in a heap of half-dry

[xv]

linen. Then there is the tale of the two lovers of Pisa, contained in Tarleton's "Newes out of Purgatorie," 1590, which is again derived from an Italian source, the "Notti" of Straparola (II., 2), where a lover is successively concealed in "a driefatte [tub] full of feathers" and other hiding places, and the husband, as before, is the lover's confidant. There are some minor touches in Tarleton's tale which suggest that Shakespeare may have had it in mind. Mrs. Quickly in one instance and Mrs. Page in another, use precisely the same expressions as Tarleton. Moreover, Mrs. Ford's enumeration (in Act IV., Sc. 2) of the various presses, coffers, chests, trunks, wells, vaults, which her jealous spouse would search, is curiously like the list of places which the equally jealous Mutio ransacks in the "Two Lovers," and supports, if it does not justify, Dr. Farmer's view that Shakespeare took Falstaff's experiences in part from Tarleton. On the other hand, it is difficult to see why Malone thought there was a connection between "The Fisher's Wife of Brainford" in "Westward for Smelts," and anything in the "Merry Wives." Its scene is laid at Windsor, for which reason he conjectured that it "probably led Shakespeare to lay the scene of Falstaff's love adventures at Windsor." Malone should have read Fielding's paper upon Shakespeare commentators. Surely the fact that the court of the "radiant Queen" mentioned in Act V. was at Windsor was probably reason enough for the choice of that place as the scene of a play written by command of her Majesty — to say nothing of the fact that Windsor appears also to have been a place (as may be seen from Tighe and

Davis's "Annals") with which Shakespeare was specially familiar, and might naturally be expected to select for an up-to-date performance. Again, was it not at Windsor that he found that sombre and picturesque legend of "Herne the Hunter," haunting the ancient oak by Queen Elizabeth's walk upon which he had hanged himself, and so secured an unexpected immortality? Apart from its solution of the Anne Page courtship, the fairy scene in the final act is the most charming of them all — "full," says one writer, "of the aromatic wood scents of Windsor Park by night," and we should be thankful that the author of "A Midsummer Night's Dream" took the trouble to invent it himself.

From the very nature of the case, many of the characters of the play, in addition to Falstaff, are revivals of personages whom the author had already staged. Justice Shallow, with Lucy's "dozen white luces" in his coat, is our old friend from the Second Part of "Henry IV.," who discoursed so admirably of Old Double's death. "He shot a fine shoot: — John of Gaunt loved him well, and betted much money on his head." One can almost hear the weak, piping voice. He still brags of his wild "swinge buckler days," when he was called "lusty Shallow," for all that he looked, according to Falstaff, like "a man made after supper of a cheese-paring"— "a forked radish, with a head fantastically carved." "I have seen the time," he says in the "Merry Wives," "with my long sword, I would have made you four tall fellows skip like rats." But he "has lived fourscore years, and upward," which makes one wonder how old

he was when he lent Sir John the thousand pounds.
From the Second Part of "Henry IV.," too, comes
Ancient Pistol with his "red lattice phrases" and "cat-
a-mountain looks," enriching the language with the memorable "Convey, the wise it call," and his immortal "The
world's mine oyster, Which I with sword will open";
and Mrs. Quickly, not yet his wife, nor easily to be identified with the worthy Hostess of the Boar's Head in East-
cheap, whom Falstaff had once sworn to marry "upon a
parcel-gilt goblet, sitting in her Dolphin chamber, at the
round table, by a sea-coal fire, upon Wednesday in Whit-
sun-week," when the prince had broken his head for liking
his father to a singing man of Windsor. In the "Merry
Wives" she does not even know Falstaff; she is, apparently, an unmarried woman-of-all-work to Caius, and has,
so far, baffled the commentators. Bardolph, the "withered
serving-man" turned tapster, with the bottle nose, and the
face that was such bad security, is also in the earlier plays.
Nym comes from "Henry V." alone, a circumstance which
goes to confirm the conclusion that the "Merry Wives"
was composed after that play; and if his "humours" be in
any way connected with Ben Jonson's comedy, can hardly
have come into existence until after 1596. Indeed, in
1598, Shakespeare himself acted in "Every Man in his
Humour," although the part he took is not known.

Dr. Brandes is probably right in assuming that the
Welch priest, Sir Hugh Evans, and the French doctor,
Caius, were concessions to the mirth-making of a purist
court which prided itself on its parts of speech, and must
have been hugely diverted by what Mrs. Quickly calls

the abusing, on either side, of the King's English. " Good worts ! good cabbage," says Falstaff of Sir Hugh ; and he flames out again even in the height of his own discomfiture. " Seese and putter ! have I lived to stand at the taunt of one that makes fritters of English ? " It is possible, also, as has indeed been suggested, that Evans with his " hung, hang, hog," and the " Jenny's case " which has furnished a motto to Rossetti, is a memory of the old days of Stratford school and the *Sententiæ Pueriles*, in which case we may see in little *William* Page the earlier *William* Shakespeare. Of the remaining characters, the handsome, hearty, buxom English wives, the jovial Host, the jealous Ford, " sweet Anne Page " and her pleasant lover, Master Fenton, whom we respect too much to believe that he really companied " with the wild Prince and Poins," — there is not much to say, or rather there is not much that need be said, beyond the fact that they come straight from contemporary life, and represent, as the characters of none other of Shakespeare's comedies represent, the types their creator found about him, in the last years of the reign of Elizabeth, when, in plain prose, and a fortnight's space, he sat down to perform the difficult task which that " radiant " but arbitrary monarch had imposed upon him, of exhibiting Falstaff in love.

The " Merry Wives " bears everywhere about it the traces of its origin. Rapid, animated, full of invention and movement, it is also packed with anachronisms, minor lapses, omissions, and discrepancies, which the piety of commentators has striven hopelessly to straighten out and reconcile, without success. And the hero is like the great

piece, — a Falstaff to order, a Falstaff of farce, a Falstaff playing a part, in whom it is scarcely possible to recognise the old ironical, cynical, resourceful, quick-witted, inimitable Falstaff of "Henry IV." Admit that the apparent ready response of the "Merry Wives" to his addresses had so befooled him as to make him lose all his knowledge of human nature and all his native shrewdness, it is scarcely possible to imagine him blundering into the simple traps that are laid for him, without suspicion. And a Falstaff that believes in fairies is not conceivable. Indeed, he says as much himself. It was the "sudden surprise of his powers" that "drove the grossness of the foppery into a received belief, in despite of the teeth of all rhyme and reason." "Have I laid my brain in the sun, and dried it," — he says again, — "that it wants matter to prevent such gross o'er-reaching as this?" Yet Shakespeare, placing him in a false position and a forced environment, could not entirely divest him of his former attributes. It is the old Falstaff who brags to "Master Brook" of the conquest he has never made; who consoles himself that his "admirable dexterity of wit" in counterfeiting the action of an old woman had saved him from discovery under the cudgel of Ford; it is the old Falstaff who gives that unrivalled description of his experiences in the buck-basket, "compassed, like a good bilbo in the circumference of a peck, hilt to point, heel to head"; —who tells Mrs. Ford, with such a martial manliness, that "he cannot cog, and say she is this and that, like a many of those lisping hawthorn buds, that come like women in men's apparel, and smell like Bucklersbury in simple time " ; — who fears when the court hear how he has been transformed and cudgelled, they will melt him out of his fat, drop by drop, to liquor fishermen's boots with, — and who has never prospered since he foreswore himself at *primero*.   It is the old Falstaff with whom no one can ever be angry, and who is never angry with any one ; who will be the life and soul of the party at Page's after the play, and will never pay that twenty pounds which he owes to " Master Brook."

AUSTIN DOBSON.

DRAMATIS PERSONÆ [1]

Sir John Falstaff.

Fenton, a gentleman.

Shallow, a country justice.

Slender, cousin to Shallow.

Ford, } two gentlemen dwelling at Windsor.
Page, }

William Page, a boy, son to Page.

Sir Hugh Evans, a Welsh parson.

Doctor Caius, a French physician.

Host of the Garter Inn.

Bardolph, }
Pistol, } sharpers attending on Falstaff.
Nym, }

Robin, page to Falstaff.

Simple, servant to Slender.

Rugby, servant to Doctor Caius.

Mistress Ford.

Mistress Page.

Anne Page, her daughter.

Mistress Quickly, servant to Doctor Caius.

Servants to Page, Ford, etc.

Scene — *Windsor, and the neighbourhood*

[1] An imperfect sketch of this play was first published in quarto in 1602, and was reissued in 1619. A complete version first appeared in the First Folio of 1623, and this was reissued in a Third Quarto in 1630. The Folio first divided the text into acts and scenes. But there is no list of "dramatis personæ." This was first supplied by Nicholas Rowe in his edition of Shakespeare's works, 1709.

ACT FIRST — SCENE I — WINDSOR
BEFORE PAGE'S HOUSE

Enter JUSTICE SHALLOW, SLENDER, *and* SIR HUGH EVANS

SHALLOW

IR HUGH, PERSUADE me not; I will make a Star-chamber matter of it: if he were twenty Sir John Falstaffs, he shall not abuse Robert Shallow, esquire.

SLEN. In the county of Gloucester, justice of peace and "Coram."

SHAL. Ay, cousin Slender, and "Custalorum."

SLEN. Ay, and "Rato-lorum" too; and a gentleman born, master parson; who writes himself "Armigero," in any bill, warrant, quittance, or obligation, "Armigero."

---

1 *Star-chamber matter*] Matter for the Court of Star Chamber, which had cognizance of all riots. Cf. Jonson's *Magnetic Lady*, III, 3: "There is a court above, of the star-chamber, To punish routs and riots."

[3]

SHAL. Ay, that I do; and have done any time these 10 three hundred years.

SLEN. All his successors gone before him hath done't; and all his ancestors that come after him may: they may give the dozen white luces in their coat.

SHAL. It is an old coat.

EVANS. The dozen white louses do become an old coat well; it agrees well, passant; it is a familiar beast to man, and signifies love.

SHAL. The luce is the fresh fish; the salt fish is an old coat.

SLEN. I may quarter, coz.

5 *"Coram"*] Slender here and in his next speech is confusedly recalling the official Latin titles of a justice of the peace. The word "quorum," which he mispronounces "coram," was prominent in the formal commission, which also designated a justice "custos rotulorum." Justice Shallow would sign his attestations "*Coram* me Roberto Shallow, *armigero*" (*i. e.* arms-bearer, esquire).

14 *dozen white luces*] "Luce" was the name commonly applied to a full-grown and ageing pike. Shallow is a caricature sketch of Sir Thomas *Lucy* of Charlecote, who is reputed to have punished Shakespeare in his youth for poaching in his park. Sir Thomas bore on his heraldic shield three *luces* hauriant argent.

16 *louses*] Sir Hugh's punning confusion of "luce" with "louse" ("a familiar beast to man") implies that he pronounced the two words alike.

19, 20 These lines are difficult to explain. Shallow, by way of denying Evans's suggestion of agreement between "luces" and "an old coat," points out that the pike, which lives in *fresh* water, can have no staleness about it; such an attribute is only possible in *salted* fish (of the sea), which can therefore be alone identified with an old cast-off coat.

21 *quarter*] Like "coat" (l. 14) and "passant" (l. 17), "quarter" is a

SHAL. You may, by marrying.

EVANS. It is marring indeed, if he quarter it.

SHAL. Not a whit.

EVANS. Yes, py 'r lady; if he has a quarter of your coat, there is but three skirts for yourself, in my simple conjectures: but that is all one. If Sir John Falstaff have committed disparagements unto you, I am of the church, and will be glad to do my benevolence to make atonements and compremises between you. 30

SHAL. The council shall hear it; it is a riot.

EVANS. It is not meet the council hear a riot; there is no fear of Got in a riot: the council, look you, shall desire to hear the fear of Got, and not to hear a riot; take your vizaments in that.

SHAL. Ha! o' my life, if I were young again, the sword should end it.

EVANS. It is petter that friends is the sword, and end it: and there is also another device in my prain, which peradventure prings goot discretions with it:— 40 there is Anne Page, which is daughter to Master Thomas Page, which is pretty virginity.

---

technical term in heraldry; used as a verb, it means to fill a compartment of a shield with armorial bearings other than those of one's father — e. g. those of one's wife.

31 *council*] the star-chamber, which was a committee of the privy council. Cf. l. 1, *supra*.

34–35 *take . . . that*] be sure of that. "Vizaments" is a blunder for "advisements" counsels, deliberations.

41 *Thomas Page*] This is the original reading. Elsewhere, II, i, 133 and 141, and V, v, 189, Page is called "George." "Thomas" is probably an oversight of the author.

[5]

SLEN. Mistress Anne Page? She has brown hair, and speaks small like a woman.

EVANS. It is that fery person for all the orld, as just as you will desire; and seven hundred pounds of moneys, and gold and silver, is her grandsire upon his death's-bed (Got deliver to a joyful resurrections!) give, when she is able to overtake seventeen years old: it were a goot motion if we leave our pribbles and prabbles, and desire a marriage between Master Abra- 50 ham and Mistress Anne Page.

SLEN. Did her grandsire leave her seven hundred pound?

EVANS. Ay, and her father is make her a petter penny.

SLEN. I know the young gentlewoman; she has good gifts.

EVANS. Seven hundred pounds and possibilities is goot gifts.

SHAL. Well, let us see honest Master Page. Is Falstaff there?

EVANS. Shall I tell you a lie? I do despise a liar as 60 I do despise one that is false, or as I despise one that is not true. The knight, Sir John, is there; and, I beseech you, be ruled by your well-willers. I will peat the door for Master Page. [Knocks] What, hoa! Got pless your house here!

PAGE. [Within] Who's there?

---

44 *speaks small*] speaks in a low voice. Cf. *Mids. N. Dr.*, I, ii, 43.

50 *pribbles and prabbles*] The Welshman's mispronunciation of bribble-brabble, a common reduplicated form of "brabble," discordant babble, vain chatter. Cf. *infra*, IV, i, 45, and V, v, 153.

Enter PAGE

EVANS. Here is Got's plessing, and your friend, and Justice Shallow; and here young Master Slender, that peradventures shall tell you another tale, if matters grow to your likings.

PAGE. I am glad to see your worships well. I thank 70 you for my venison, Master Shallow.

SHAL. Master Page, I am glad to see you: much good do it your good heart! I wished your venison better; it was ill killed. How doth good Mistress Page? — and I thank you always with my heart, la! with my heart.

PAGE. Sir, I thank you.

SHAL. Sir, I thank you; by yea and no, I do.

PAGE. I am glad to see you, good Master Slender.

SLEN. How does your fallow greyhound, sir? I heard say he was outrun on Cotsall.   80

PAGE. It could not be judged, sir.

SLEN. You 'll not confess, you 'll not confess.

SHAL. That he will not. 'T is your fault; 't is your fault; 't is a good dog.

PAGE. A cur, sir.

SHAL. Sir, he 's a good dog, and a fair dog: can there be more said? he is good and fair. Is Sir John Falstaff here?

---

80 *Cotsall*] The local pronunciation of Cotswold. On the Cotswold hills, in Gloucestershire, coursing matches and meetings for rural sports were frequently held. The district was within easy distance of Stratford-on-Avon. Cf. *2 Hen. IV*, III, ii, 20: " Will Squele, a *Cotswold* man."

[7]

PAGE. Sir, he is within; and I would I could do a good office between you.

EVANS. It is spoke as a Christians ought to speak.   90

SHAL. He hath wronged me, Master Page.

PAGE. Sir, he doth in some sort confess it.

SHAL. If it be confessed, it is not redressed: is not that so, Master Page? He hath wronged me; indeed he hath; at a word, he hath, believe me: Robert Shallow, esquire, saith, he is wronged.

PAGE. Here comes Sir John.

Enter SIR JOHN FALSTAFF, BARDOLPH, NYM, *and* PISTOL

FAL. Now, Master Shallow, you 'll complain of me to the king?

SHAL. Knight, you have beaten my men, killed my deer, and broke open my lodge.   101

FAL. But not kissed your keeper's daughter?

SHAL. Tut, a pin! this shall be answered.

FAL. I will answer it straight; I have done all this. That is now answered.

SHAL. The council shall know this.

FAL. 'T were better for you if it were known in counsel: you 'll be laughed at.

EVANS. Pauca verba, Sir John; goot worts.

FAL. Goot worts! good cabbage. Slender, I broke your head: what matter have you against me?   111

SLEN. Marry, sir, I have matter in my head against

107–108 *known in counsel*] kept secret.

110 *worts*] vegetables, of which the "cole-wort" or cabbage is one of the commonest species.

you ; and against your cony-catching rascals, Bardolph,
Nym, and Pistol.

BARD. You Banbury cheese !

SLEN. Ay, it is no matter.

PIST. How now, Mephostophilus !

SLEN. Ay, it is no matter.

NYM. Slice, I say ! pauca, pauca : slice ! that 's my
humour.   120

SLEN. Where 's Simple, my man ? Can you tell,
cousin ?

EVANS. Peace, I pray you. Now let us understand.
There is three umpires in this matter, as I understand ;
that is, Master Page, fidelicet Master Page ; and there is
myself, fidelicet myself ; and the three party is, lastly
and finally, mine host of the Garter.

PAGE. We three, to hear it and end it between them.

EVANS. Fery goot : I will make a prief of it in my
note-book ; and we will afterwards ork upon the cause
with as great discreetly as we can.   131

FAL. Pistol !

PIST. He hears with ears.

---

115 *Banbury cheese*] flat, thin cheese. Cf. *Jacke Drum's Entertainment*,
  Act III, in Simpson's *School of Shakspere*, II, 173 : " You are like
  a *Banbury cheese*, Nothing but paring."

117 *Mephostophilus*] A probable reference to Marlowe's tragedy of
  Dr. Faustus. Cf. IV, v, 64, *infra*, " Three *Doctor Faustuses*."

119 *Slice . . . pauca*] Nym echoes Evans' exclamation " pauca verba "
  of l. 109, *supra*. " Slice " is a characteristic allusion to the sword,
  and resembles Nym's hint in *Hen. V*, II, i, 22 : " Some say knives
  have edges."

EVANS. The tevil and his tam! what phrase is this, "He hears with ear"? why, it is affectations.

FAL. Pistol, did you pick Master Slender's purse?

SLEN. Ay, by these gloves, did he, or I would I might never come in mine own great chamber again else, of seven groats in mill-sixpences, and two Edward shovel-boards, that cost me two shilling and two pence a-piece of Yead Miller, by these gloves. 141

FAL. Is this true, Pistol?

EVANS. No; it is false, if it is a pick-purse.

PIST. Ha, thou mountain-foreigner! Sir John and
       master mine,
I combat challenge of this latten bilbo.
Word of denial in thy labras here!
Word of denial: froth and scum, thou liest!

SLEN. By these gloves, then, 't was he. 149

NYM. Be avised, sir, and pass good humours: I will

139-140 *seven groats . . . a-piece*] groats, *i. e.* four-penny pieces, were coins of very old standing; milled or stamped sixpences were first coined in 1561. "Edward shovel-boards," which are called "shove-groat shillings" in *2 Hen. IV*, II, iv, 182, were broad and heavy shilling-pieces of Edward VI's reign, and came to be used as counters or discs in the popular game of shovel-board, which in principle resembles the more modern game of "squaylea." Slender's words indicate that the value of Edward VI's shillings had greatly appreciated; but his figures are not to be depended on. Seven groats (of four-pence each) could not be converted into sixpence's.

141 *Yead*] A colloquial form of Ned.

146 *latten bilbo*] Slender is compared to a sword blade; cf. III, v, 98, *infra*.

147 *labras*] Pistol bombastically uses the Spanish word for lips.

150-151 *I will say "marry trap"*] I will catch you (cry quits with you), if you play the "nuthook" (*i. e.* constable or catchpole) with me.

say "marry trap" with you, if you run the nuthook's humour on me; that is the very note of it.

SLEN. By this hat, then, he in the red face had it; for though I cannot remember what I did when you made me drunk, yet I am not altogether an ass.

FAL. What say you, Scarlet and John?

BARD. Why, sir, for my part, I say the gentleman had drunk himself out of his five sentences.

EVANS. It is his five senses: fie, what the ignorance is!

BARD. And being fap, sir, was, as they say, cashiered; and so conclusions passed the careires.   161

SLEN. Ay, you spake in Latin then too; but 't is no matter: I 'll ne'er be drunk whilst I live again, but in honest, civil, godly company, for this trick: if I be drunk, I 'll be drunk with those that have the fear of God, and not with drunken knaves.

EVANS. So Got udge me, that is a virtuous mind.

FAL. You hear all these matters denied, gentlemen; you hear it.

Enter ANNE PAGE, *with wine;* MISTRESS FORD *and* MISTRESS
PAGE, *following*

PAGE. Nay, daughter, carry the wine in; we 'll drink within.   [*Exit Anne Page.*   171

---

156 *Scarlet and John*] The names of two followers of Robin Hood. "Scarlet" alludes to Bardolph's red face.

160 *fap*] drunken; probably from "vappa," a drunken person.

161 *passed the careires*] galloped on at full speed; a technical term of the equestrian menage, or art of riding. Cf. *Hen. V*, II, i, 123.

SLEN. O heaven! this is Mistress Anne Page.

PAGE. How now, Mistress Ford!

FAL. Mistress Ford, by my troth, you are very well met: by your leave, good mistress. [*Kisses her.*

PAGE. Wife, bid these gentlemen welcome. Come, · we have a hot venison pasty to dinner: come, gentlemen, I hope we shall drink down all unkindness.

[*Exeunt all except Shal., Slen., and Evans.*

SLEN. I had rather than forty shillings I had my Book of Songs and Sonnets here. 180

Enter SIMPLE

How now, Simple! where have you been? I must wait on myself, must I? You have not the Book of Riddles about you, have you?

SIM. Book of Riddles! why, did you not lend it to Alice Shortcake upon All-hallowmas last, a fortnight afore Michaelmas?

---

180 *Book of Songs and Sonnets*] Slender seeks amatory verse wherewith to court Anne Page. The book he specifies is probably the popular poetic miscellany, generally called *Tottel's Miscellany*, but really entitled *Songes and Sonnettes*, 1557. An eighth edition appeared in 1587.

182 *Book of Riddles*] *The Booke of Mery Riddles* was very popular in the 16th and 17th centuries, though no edition earlier than that of 1600 seems to be extant.

185–186 *All-hallowmas last . . . Michaelmas*] Slender seems to confuse Michaelmas (29 September) with Martlemas or Martinmas (11 November). All-hallowmas (All Saints, 1 November) comes some five weeks after Michaelmas, but ten days "afore" Martlemas.

[12]

SHAL. Come, coz; come, coz; we stay for you. A
word with you, coz; marry, this, coz: there is, as 't were,
a tender, a kind of tender, made afar off by Sir Hugh
here. Do you understand me?   190

SLEN. Ay, sir, you shall find me reasonable; if it be
so, I shall do that that is reason.

SHAL. Nay, but understand me.

SLEN. So I do, sir.

EVANS. Give ear to his motions, Master Slender: I
will description the matter to you, if you be capacity
of it.

SLEN. Nay, I will do as my cousin Shallow says: I
pray you, pardon me; he's a justice of peace in his
country, simple though I stand here.

EVANS. But that is not the question: the question is
concerning your marriage.   201

SHAL. Ay, there's the point, sir.

EVANS. Marry, is it; the very point of it; to Mistress
Anne Page.

SLEN. Why, if it be so, I will marry her upon any
reasonable demands.

EVANS. But can you affection the 'oman? Let us
command to know that of your mouth or of your lips;
for divers philosophers hold that the lips is parcel of the
mouth. Therefore, precisely, can you carry your good
will to the maid?   211

SHAL. Cousin Abraham Slender, can you love her?

SLEN. I hope, sir, I will do as it shall become one
that would do reason.

EVANS. Nay, Got's lords and his ladies! you must

speak possitable, if you can carry her your desires towards her.

SHAL. That you must. Will you, upon good dowry, marry her?

SLEN. I will do a greater thing than that, upon your request, cousin, in any reason. 221

SHAL. Nay, conceive me, conceive me, sweet coz: what I do is to pleasure you, coz. Can you love the maid?

SLEN. I will marry her, sir, at your request: but if there be no great love in the beginning, yet heaven may decrease it upon better acquaintance, when we are married and have more occasion to know one another; I hope, upon familiarity will grow more contempt: but if you say, "Marry her," I will marry her; that I am freely dissolved, and dissolutely.

EVANS. It is a fery discretion answer; save the fall is in the ort "dissolutely:" the ort is, according to our meaning, "resolutely:" his meaning is good. 232

SHAL. Ay, I think my cousin meant well.

SLEN. Ay, or else I would I might be hanged, la!

SHAL. Here comes fair Mistress Anne.

Re-enter ANNE PAGE

Would I were young for your sake, Mistress Anne!

ANNE. The dinner is on the table; my father desires your worships' company.

230-231 *fall* . . . *ort*] Fall is a mispronunciation of "fault," as "ort" is of "word."

SHAL. I will wait on him, fair Mistress Anne.

EVANS. Od's plessed will! I will not be absence at
the grace.   [*Exeunt Shallow and Evans.* 241

ANNE. Will 't please your worship to come in, sir?

SLEN. No, I thank you, forsooth, heartily; I am very
well.

ANNE. The dinner attends you, sir.

SLEN. I am not a-hungry, I thank you, forsooth.
Go, sirrah, for all you are my man, go wait upon my
cousin Shallow. [*Exit Simple.*] A justice of peace sometime may be beholding to his friend for a man. I keep
but three men and a boy yet, till my mother be dead: but
what though? yet I live like a poor gentleman born. 251

ANNE. I may not go in without your worship: they
will not sit till you come.

SLEN. I' faith, I 'll eat nothing; I thank you as much
as though I did.

ANNE. I pray you, sir, walk in.

SLEN. I had rather walk here, I thank you. I
bruised my shin th' other day with playing at sword and
dagger with a master of fence; three veneys for a dish
of stewed prunes; and, by my troth, I cannot abide the
smell of hot meat since. Why do your dogs bark so?
be there bears i' the town?   262

ANNE. I think there are, sir; I heard them talked of.

259–260] *three veneys . . . prunes*] The wager for which the fencing-
   match was played was a dish of stewed prunes to be paid to him
   who scored three "veneys" (*i. e.* hits). Florio in his *Italian-English
   Dictionary* (*s. v.*, "Tocco, a touch") explains "a *venie* at fence" to
   be "a hit."

[15]

SLEN. I love the sport well; but I shall as soon quarrel at it as any man in England. You are afraid, if you see the bear loose, are you not?

ANNE. Ay, indeed, sir.

SLEN. That's meat and drink to me, now. I have seen Sackerson loose twenty times, and have taken him by the chain; but, I warrant you, the women have so cried and shrieked at it, that it passed: but women, indeed, cannot abide 'em; they are very ill-favoured rough things. 272

Re-enter PAGE

PAGE. Come, gentle Master Slender, come; we stay for you.

SLEN. I'll eat nothing, I thank you, sir.

PAGE. By cock and pie, you shall not choose, sir! come, come.

SLEN. Nay, pray you, lead the way.

PAGE. Come on, sir.

SLEN. Mistress Anne, yourself shall go first. 280

ANNE. Not I, sir; pray you, keep on.

SLEN. Truly, I will not go first; truly, la! I will not do you that wrong.

268 *meat and drink*] a common proverbial phrase, expressing infinite satisfaction. Cf. *As you like it*, V, i, 10: "It is *meat and drink* to me to see a clown."

269 *Sackerson*] The name of a far-famed performing bear, which was a chief attraction, at the date of the performance of this play, at the Paris Garden in Southwark. Sir John Davies in No. xliii of his *Epigrams* (published about 1596) describes a law-student forsaking his law-books "to see . . . *Sacarson*."

ANNE. I pray you, sir.

SLEN. I 'll rather be unmannerly than troublesome. You do yourself wrong, indeed, la! [*Exeunt.*

SCENE II—THE SAME

Enter SIR HUGH EVANS *and* SIMPLE

EVANS. Go your ways, and ask of Doctor Caius' house which is the way : and there dwells one Mistress Quickly, which is in the manner of his nurse, or his dry nurse, or his cook, or his laundry, his washer, and his wringer.

SIM. Well, sir.

EVANS. Nay, it is petter yet. Give her this letter ; for it is a 'oman that altogether's acquaintance with Mistress Anne Page : and the letter is, to desire and require her to solicit your master's desires to Mistress Anne Page. I pray you, be gone : I will make an end 10 of my dinner ; there 's pippins and cheese to come.

[*Exeunt.*

SCENE III — A ROOM IN THE GARTER INN

Enter FALSTAFF, HOST, BARDOLPH, NYM, PISTOL, *and* ROBIN

FAL. Mine host of the Garter !

HOST. What says my bully-rook ? speak scholarly and wisely.

7 *that altogether's acquaintance*] that is fully acquainted with.

2

Fal. Truly, mine host, I must turn away some of my followers.

Host. Discard, bully Hercules ; cashier : let them wag ; trot, trot.

Fal. I sit at ten pounds a week.

Host. Thou 'rt an emperor, Cæsar, Keisar, and Phee- zar. I will entertain Bardolph ; he shall draw, he shall 10 tap : said I well, bully Hector?

Fal. Do so, good mine host.

Host. I have spoke ; let him follow. [*To Bard.*] Let me see thee froth and lime: I am at a word ; follow.

[*Exit.*

Fal. Bardolph, follow him. A tapster is a good trade : an old cloak makes a new jerkin ; a withered serving-man a fresh tapster. Go ; adieu.

Bard. It is a life that I have desired: I will thrive.

Pist. O base Hungarian wight ! wilt thou the spigot wield? [*Exit Bardolph.* 20

---

14 *froth and lime*] The host invites Bardolph to try his hand as a tapster, whose function it was to make the beer "froth and lime," *i. e.* sparkle by covertly introducing *lime* into the glass. Cf. *1 Hen. IV*, II, iv, 117, "Here 's *lime* in this sack," and 119, "a cup of sack with *lime* in it." *At a word*, used adverbially, ordinarily means "in fine," "to sum up," "in short." Here the sense seems to be, "I am as good as my word."

19 *Hungarian*] The earlier Quartos read *Gongarian*. Steevens quoted without reference a line from an unidentified old play, "O base Gongarian ! wilt thou the distaff wield?" But the epithet "Hungarian" was often used in the sense of "swaggering" or "bombastic."

NYM. He was gotten in drink: is not the humour conceited?

FAL. I am glad I am so acquit of this tinder-box: his thefts were too open; his filching was like an unskilful singer; he kept not time.

NYM. The good humour is to steal at a minute's rest.

PIST. "Convey," the wise it call. "Steal!" foh! a fico for the phrase!

FAL. Well, sirs, I am almost out at heels.

PIST. Why, then, let kibes ensue.   30

FAL. There is no remedy; I must cony-catch; I must shift.

PIST. Young ravens must have food.

FAL. Which of you know Ford of this town?

PIST. I ken the wight: he is of substance good.

FAL. My honest lads, I will tell you what I am about.

PIST. Two yards, and more.

FAL. No quips now, Pistol! Indeed, I am in the waist two yards about; but I am now about no waste; I am about thrift. Briefly, I do mean to make love to 40 Ford's wife: I spy entertainment in her; she discourses, she carves, she gives the leer of invitation: I can construe the action of her familiar style; and the hardest

---

26 *at a minute's rest*] This, the original reading, has been ingeniously altered by many editors to *at a minim's rest*. "Minim" is the shortest note in music. "At a minim's rest" would mean "with the utmost rapidity." The emendation is supported by *Rom. and Jul.* II, iv, 22: "He rests me his *minim rest*," in Mercutio's description of Tybalt's method of fight.

voice of her behaviour, to be Englished rightly, is, "I am Sir John Falstaff's."

PIST. He hath studied her will, and translated her will, out of honesty into English.

NYM. The anchor is deep: will that humour pass?

FAL. Now, the report goes she has all the rule of her husband's purse: he hath a legion of angels.   50

PIST. As many devils entertain; and "To her, boy," say I.

NYM. The humour rises; it is good: humour me the angels.

FAL. I have writ me here a letter to her: and here another to Page's wife, who even now gave me good eyes too, examined my parts with most judicious œillades; sometimes the beam of her view gilded my foot, sometimes my portly belly.

PIST. Then did the sun on dunghill shine.   60

NYM. I thank thee for that humour.

FAL. O, she did so course o'er my exteriors with such a greedy intention, that the appetite of her eye did seem to scorch me up like a burning-glass! Here's another letter to her: she bears the purse too; she is a region

---

46–47 *will* . . . *will*] This is the reading of the First Folio. The earlier Quartos read *well* for the first *will* and omit the second phrase. *Will* in both cases is doubtless right.

57 *œillades*] A French word meaning "amorous glances," very occasionally met with in Elizabethan literature.

65–66 *a region in Guiana*] An allusion to Sir Walter Ralegh's recent exploration of Guiana, of which he published an account in 1595.

in Guiana, all gold and bounty.   I will be cheaters to
them both, and they shall be exchequers to me; they
shall be my East and West Indies, and I will trade to
them both.   Go bear thou this letter to Mistress Page;
and thou this to Mistress Ford: we will thrive, lads, we 70
will thrive.

PIST. Shall I Sir Pandarus of Troy become,
And by my side wear steel? then, Lucifer take all!

NYM. I will run no base humour: here, take the
humour-letter: I will keep the haviour of reputation.

FAL. [*To Robin*] Hold, sirrah, bear you these letters
          tightly;
Sail like my pinnace to these golden shores.
Rogues, hence, avaunt! vanish like hailstones, go;
Trudge, plod away o' the hoof; seek shelter, pack!
Falstaff will learn the humour of the age,   80
French thrift, you rogues; myself and skirted page.
          [*Exeunt Falstaff and Robin.*

PIST. Let vultures gripe thy guts! for gourd and
          fullam holds,
And high and low beguiles the rich and poor:
Tester I'll have in pouch when thou shalt lack,
Base Phrygian Turk!

NYM. I have operations which be humours of revenge.

PIST. Wilt thou revenge?

---

66 *cheaters*] A punning quibble on "cheaters" and "escheaters,"
      officers of the Exchequer.
82–83 *gourd . . . low*] "Gourd," "fullam," "high [men]" and "low
      [men]" were all cant terms for loaded dice in common use by
      sharpers.

NYM. By welkin and her star!
PIST. With wit or steel?
NYM. With both the humours, I: 90
I will discuss the humour of this love to Page.
PIST. And I to Ford shall eke unfold
        How Falstaff, varlet vile,
    His dove will prove, his gold will hold,
        And his soft couch defile.
NYM. My humour shall not cool: I will incense Page
to deal with poison; I will possess him with yellowness,
for the revolt of mine is dangerous: that is my true
humour.
PIST. Thou art the Mars of malecontents: I second
thee; troop on.   [*Exeunt.* 100

SCENE IV—A ROOM IN DOCTOR CAIUS'S HOUSE

Enter MISTRESS QUICKLY, SIMPLE, *and* RUGBY

QUICK. What, John Rugby! I pray thee, go to the
casement, and see if you can see my master, Master
Doctor Caius, coming. If he do, i' faith, and find any

---

97 *yellowness*] the traditional colour of jealousy.
98 *revolt of mine*] This is the original reading. Theobald suggested
    revolt of mien (*i. e.* change of complexion), which does not add
    much point to Nym's threat. The Cambridge editors suggest
    that "anger" is omitted after "mine." Most probably Nym
    merely means to say in his grandiloquent jargon "my revolt,"
    i. e. "my purpose of renouncing allegiance to Falstaff."

body in the house, here will be an old abusing of God's
patience and the king's English.

RUG. I 'll go watch.

QUICK. Go; and we 'll have a posset for 't soon at night,
in faith, at the latter end of a sea-coal fire. [*Exit Rugby.*]
An honest, willing, kind fellow, as ever servant shall
come in house withal; and, I warrant you, no tell-tale 10
nor no breed-bate : his worst fault is, that he is given to
prayer; he is something peevish that way : but nobody
but has his fault ; but let that pass.   Peter Simple, you
say your name is ?

SIM. Ay, for fault of a better.

QUICK. And Master Slender 's your master ?

SIM. Ay, forsooth.

QUICK. Does he not wear a great round beard, like a
glover's paring-knife ?

SIM. No, forsooth : he hath but a little wee face, with 20
a little yellow beard, — a Cain-coloured beard.

QUICK. A softly-sprighted man, is he not ?

---

20 *wee face*] This is the original reading. Capell needlessly substituted
whey-face (meaning " pale-faced "), as in *Macb.*, V, iii, 17.   In the
Second Quarto (in the preceding speech, which the Folio alters),
Dame Quickly applies to Slender's beard the epithet "whay
coloured," but *wee* is quite appropriate to the context.

21 *Cain-coloured*] The early Quartos read " *Kane* colored," which tends
to justify the popular emendation " *Cane*-coloured " for the First
Folio reading " *Caine*-colored."   " Cane-coloured beard " would
be much the same as "straw-colour beard " in *Mids. N. Dr.*, I,
ii, 82.   If " *Cain*-coloured " be retained, there would be a reference to the red colour of Cain's beard in current pictorial illustra-
tions of Scriptural history.

[23]

SIM. Ay, forsooth: but he is as tall a man of his hands as any is between this and his head; he hath fought with a warrener.

QUICK. How say you?—O, I should remember him: does he not hold up his head, as it were, and strut in his gait?

SIM. Yes, indeed, does he.

QUICK. Well, heaven send Anne Page no worse fortune! Tell Master Parson Evans I will do what I can so for your master: Anne is a good girl, and I wish —

Re-enter RUGBY

RUG. Out, alas! here comes my master.

QUICK. We shall all be shent. Run in here, good young man; go into this closet: he will not stay long. [*Shuts Simple in the closet.*] What, John Rugby! John! what, John, I say! Go, John, go inquire for my master; I doubt he be not well, that he comes not home.

[*Singing*] And down, down, adown-a, &c.

Enter DOCTOR CAIUS

CAIUS. Vat is you sing? I do not like des toys. Pray you, go and vetch me in my closet un boitier vert,—a box, a green-a box: do intend vat I speak? a green-a box.

---

23 *as tall a man of his hands*] In Florio's *Italian Dictionary*, 1598, "manesco" is interpreted as "readie or nimble-handed; *a tall man of his hands*."

QUICK. Ay, forsooth; I'll fetch it you. [*Aside*] I am glad he went not in himself: if he had found the young man, he would have been horn-mad.

CAIUS. Fe, fe, fe, fe! ma foi, il fait fort chaud. Je m'en vais à la cour, — la grande affaire.

QUICK. Is it this, sir?

CAIUS. Oui; mette le au mon pocket: dépêcne, quickly. Vere is dat knave Rugby?

QUICK. What, John Rugby! John!   50

RUG. Here, Sir!

CAIUS. You are John Rugby, and you are Jack Rugby. Come, take-a your rapier, and come after my heel to the court.

RUG. 'T is ready, sir, here in the porch.

CAIUS. By my trot, I tarry too long. Od's me! Qu'ai-j'oublié! dere is some simples in my closet, dat I vill not for the varld I shall leave behind.

QUICK. Ay me, he'll find the young man there, and be mad!   60

CAIUS. O diable, diable! vat is in my closet? Villain! larron! [*Pulling Simple out.*] Rugby, my rapier!

QUICK. Good master, be content.

CAIUS. Wherefore shall I be content-a?

QUICK. The young man is an honest man.

CAIUS. What shall de honest man do in my closet? dere is no honest man dat shall come in my closet.

QUICK. I beseech you, be not so phlegmatic. Here the truth of it: he came of an errand to me from Parson Hugh.

CAIUS. Vell.   70

[25]

SIM. Ay, forsooth; to desire her to —

QUICK. Peace, I pray you.

CAIUS. Peace-a your tongue. Speak-a your tale.

SIM. To desire this honest gentlewoman, your maid, to speak a good word to Mistress Anne Page for my master in the way of marriage.

QUICK. This is all, indeed, la! but I'll ne'er put my finger in the fire, and need not.

CAIUS. Sir Hugh send-a you? Rugby, baille me some paper. Tarry you a little-a while. [*Writes.* 80

QUICK. [*Aside to Simple*] I am glad he is so quiet: if he had been throughly moved, you should have heard him so loud and so melancholy. But notwithstanding, man, I'll do you your master what good I can: and the very yea and the no is, the French doctor, my master, — I may call him my master, look you, for I keep his house; and I wash, wring, brew, bake, scour, dress meat and drink, make the beds, and do all myself, —

SIM. [*Aside to Quickly*] 'Tis a great charge to come under one body's hand. 90

QUICK. [*Aside to Simple*] Are you avised o' that? you shall find it a great charge: and to be up early and down late;— but notwithstanding,— to tell you in your ear; I would have no words of it,— my master himself is in love with Mistress Anne Page: but not-withstanding that, I know Anne's mind,—that's neither here nor there.

CAIUS. You jack'nape, give-a this letter to Sir Hugh;

79 *baille*] French for " give, deliver."

by gar, it is a shallenge: I will cut his troat in de park;
and I will teach a scurvy jack-a-nape priest to meddle
or make.   You may be gone; it is not good you tarry
here. —By gar, I will cut all his two stones; by gar, he
shall not have a stone to throw at his dog. [*Exit Simple.* 103

QUICK. Alas, he speaks but for his friend.

CAIUS. It is no matter-a ver dat: —do not you tell-a
me dat I shall have Anne Page for myself? — By gar,
I vill kill de Jack priest; and I have appointed mine
host of de Jarteer to measure our weapon. — By gar, I
will myself have Anne Page.

QUICK. Sir, the maid loves you, and all shall be well.
We must give folks leave to prate: what, the good-jer!

CAIUS. Rugby, come to the court with me.   By gar,
if I have not Anne Page, I shall turn your head out of
my door.   Follow my heels, Rugby.   113

[*Exeunt Caius and Rugby.*

QUICK. You shall have An fool's-head of your own.
No, I know Anne's mind for that: never a woman in

110 *what, the good-jer!*] a common expletive expressive of surprise;
"in the name of fortune!"   A contemporary Dutch expression
(Wat goedtjaar), almost identical in form, was commonly rendered
in French translation by the phrase " Que bon heur est cela?"
This seems to prove that the English words present elliptically
some such phrase as "What good fortune, or advantage, comes of
that?" Sir Thomas Hanmer's suggestion that "good year" is a
corruption of an imaginary French word "goujeres," a venereal
disease, may safely be rejected.

114 *fool's-head . . . own*] Cf. *Mids. N. Dr.*, III, i, 106: " You see an
ass-head of your own" (you make a fool of yourself).   "An"
can only stand here for the article "a"; it perhaps indicates

Windsor knows more of Anne's mind than I do; nor
can do more than I do with her, I thank heaven.

FENT. [*Within*] Who's within there? ho!

QUICK. Who's there, I trow? Come near the house,
I pray you.   190

Enter FENTON

FENT. How now, good woman! how dost thou?

QUICK. The better that it pleases your good worship
to ask.

FENT. What news? how does pretty Mistress Anne?

QUICK. In truth, sir, and she is pretty, and honest,
and gentle; and one that is your friend, I can tell you
that by the way; I praise heaven for it.

FENT. Shall I do any good, think'st thou? shall I
not lose my suit?   129

QUICK. Troth, sir, all is in his hands above: but not-
withstanding, Master Fenton, I'll be sworn on a book,
she loves you. Have not your worship a wart above
your eye?

FENT. Yes, marry, have I; what of that?

QUICK. Well, thereby hangs a tale:—good faith, it
is such another Nan; but, I detest, an honest maid as
ever broke bread:—we had an hour's talk of that wart.
—I shall never laugh but in that maid's company!—
But, indeed, she is given too much to allicholy and
musing: but for you—well, go to.   139

that Shakespeare first wrote "ass-head," which he altered to
"fool's-head" on second thoughts.

FENT. Well, I shall see her to-day. Hold, there's money for thee; let me have thy voice in my behalf: if thou seest her before me, commend me.

QUICK. Will I? i' faith, that we will; and I will tell your worship more of the wart the next time we have confidence; and of other wooers.

FENT. Well, farewell; I am in great haste now.

QUICK. Farewell to your worship. [*Exit Fenton*] Truly, an honest gentleman: but Anne loves him not; for I know Anne's mind as well as another does. — Out upon't! what have I forgot?   [*Exit.* 184

ACT SECOND — SCENE I

BEFORE PAGE'S HOUSE

Enter MISTRESS PAGE, *with a letter*

MISTRESS PAGE

HAT, HAVE I SCAPED love-letters in the holiday-time of my beauty, and am I now a subject for them? Let me see.

[*Reads.*

" Ask me no reason why I love you; for though Love use Reason for his physician, he admits him not for his counsellor. You are not young, no more am I; go to, then, there's sympathy: you are merry, so am I; ha, ha! then there's more sympathy: you love sack, and so do I; would you desire better sympathy? Let it suffice thee, Mistress Page, — at the least, if the love of soldier can suffice, — that I love thee. I will not say, pity me, — 't is not a soldier-like phrase; but I say, love me. By me,

10

> Thine own true knight,
> By day or night,
> Or any kind of light,
> With all his might
> For thee to fight,   JOHN FALSTAFF."

What a Herod of Jewry is this! O wicked, wicked world! One that is well-nigh worn to pieces with age to show himself a young gallant! What an unweighed behaviour hath this Flemish drunkard picked — with the devil's name! — out of my conversation, that he dares in this manner assay me? Why, he hath not been thrice in my company! What should I say to him? I was then frugal of my mirth: Heaven forgive me! Why, I'll exhibit a bill in the parliament for the putting down of men. How shall I be revenged on him? for revenged I will be, as sure as his guts are made of puddings.

Enter MISTRESS FORD

MRS FORD. Mistress Page! trust me, I was going to your house.

MRS PAGE. And, trust me, I was coming to you. You look very ill.

MRS FORD. Nay, I'll ne'er believe that; I have to show to the contrary.

MRS PAGE. Faith, but you do, in my mind.

MRS FORD. Well, I do, then; yet, I say, I could show you to the contrary. O Mistress Page, give me some counsel!

MRS PAGE. What's the matter, woman?

[31]

MRS FORD. O woman, if it were not for one trifling respect, I could come to such honour!

MRS PAGE. Hang the trifle, woman! take the honour. 40 What is it?—dispense with trifles;—what is it?

MRS FORD. If I would but go to hell for an eternal moment or so, I could be knighted.

MRS PAGE. What? thou liest! Sir Alice Ford! These knights will hack; and so thou shouldst not alter the article of thy gentry.

MRS FORD. We burn daylight:—here, read, read; perceive how I might be knighted. I shall think the worse of fat men, as long as I have an eye to make difference of men's liking: and yet he would not swear; 50 praised women's modesty; and gave such orderly and well-behaved reproof to all uncomeliness, that I would

---

45 *hack*] commonly explained in the unsupported sense of "grow hackneyed," "pall," "get too common," with a reference to James I's indiscriminate creation of knights (at a date later than the first draft of the play). There seems no point in the suggestion that "hack" is used here in its ordinary sense of "mutilate," "cut off," in allusion to the ceremonial degradation of unworthy knights by cutting off their spurs, the special emblem of chivalry. "Hack" undoubtedly appears in its ordinary sense of "mutilate," *infra*, III, i, 71, but in a later scene it recurs in quite a different and apparently a ribald sense in IV, i, 60, where Mrs. Quickly says a boy is taught by his master "*to hick and to hack*, which they 'll do fast enough of themselves, and to call 'horum' (*i. e.* whore)." "Hack" or "hackney" was a slang name for a loose woman, and hence a verb meaning "to have dealings with loose women" is deducible. It is possible that Mrs. Page here intends some such quibbling allusion.

47 *We burn daylight*] Cf. *Rom. and Jul.*, I, iv, 43: "We waste our lights in vain like *lamps by day*."

have sworn his disposition would have gone to the truth of his words; but they do no more adhere and keep place together than the Hundredth Psalm to the tune of " Green Sleeves." What tempest, I trow, threw this whale, with so many tuns of oil in his belly, ashore at Windsor? How shall I be revenged on him? I think the best way were to entertain him with hope, till the wicked fire of lust have melted him in his own grease. Did you ever hear the like? 60

MRS PAGE. Letter for letter, but that the name of Page and Ford differs! To thy great comfort in this mystery of ill opinions, here's the twin-brother of thy letter: but let thine inherit first; for, I protest, mine never shall. I warrant he hath a thousand of these letters, writ with blank space for different names, — sure, more, — and these are of the second edition: he will print them, out of doubt; for he cares not what he puts into the press, when he would put us two. I had rather be a giantess, and lie under Mount Pelion. Well, I will find you twenty lascivious turtles ere one chaste man. 70

MRS FORD. Why, this is the very same; the very hand, the very words. What doth he think of us?

MRS. PAGE. Nay, I know not: it makes me almost

---

55 *the tune of " Green Sleeves"*] One of the most popular ballads of Shakespeare's day, to which reference is made again, V, v, 18, *infra*; it was licensed for print in 1580, but no copy of the original words survives, although the tune is extant. "A new courtly sonet of the Lady Greensleeves to the new *tune of Greensleeves*," one of many imitations of the original verses, figures in Robinson's *Handfull of Pleasant Delights*, 1584 (ed. Arber, p. 17).

ready to wrangle with mine own honesty. I 'll entertain myself like one that I am not acquainted withal ; for, sure, unless he know some strain in me, that I know not myself, he would never have boarded me in this fury.

MRS FORD. "Boarding," call you it ? I 'll be sure to keep him above deck. 80

MRS PAGE. So will I : if he come under my hatches, I 'll never to sea again. Let 's be revenged on him : let 's appoint him a meeting ; give him a show of comfort in his suit, and lead him on with a fine-baited delay, till he hath pawned his horses to mine host of the Garter.

MRS FORD. Nay, I will consent to act any villany against him, that may not sully the chariness of our honesty. O, that my husband saw this letter ! it would give eternal food to his jealousy.

MRS PAGE. Why, look where he comes ; and my 90 good man too : he 's as far from jealousy as I am from giving him cause ; and that, I hope, is an unmeasurable distance.

MRS FORD. You are the happier woman.

MRS PAGE. Let 's consult together against this greasy knight. Come hither. [*They retire.*

Enter FORD, *with* PISTOL, *and* PAGE, *with* NYM

FORD. Well, I hope it be not so.

PIST. Hope is a curtal dog in some affairs :
Sir John affects thy wife.

---

77 *some strain*] some natural disposition (to sensuality). Mrs. Page employs the word in the identical sense, III, iii, 163, *infra :* " I would all of the same *strain* were in the same distress."

FORD. Why, sir, my wife is not young.   100
PIST. He wooes both high and low, both rich and poor,
Both young and old, one with another, Ford;
He loves the gallimaufry: Ford, perpend.
FORD. Love my wife!
PIST. With liver burning hot. Prevent, or go thou,
Like Sir Actæon he, with Ringwood at thy heels:
O, odious is the name!
FORD. What name, sir?
PIST. The horn, I say. Farewell.   109
Take heed; have open eye; for thieves do foot by night:
Take heed, ere summer comes, or cuckoo-birds do sing.
Away, Sir Corporal Nym!—
Believe it, Page; he speaks sense.   [*Exit.*
FORD. [*Aside*] I will be patient; I will find out this.
NYM. [*To Page*] And this is true; I like not the hu-
mour of lying. He hath wronged me in some humours:

---

103 *gallimaufry*] This word, which is from the French, properly means
  " a stew or hash" of mixed meats. Pistol applies it to a promis-
  cuous assembly of persons.
106 *Sir Actæon . . . Ringwood*] The story of Actæon, an ardent hunter,
  who for defying Diana, goddess of the chase, was turned by her
  into a stag, is told by Ovid, *Met.*, III, 138, *seq.* Ovid gives the
  names of Actæon's hounds, the last being called " Hylactor."
  Golding, in his translation of Ovid's *Metamorphoses*, renders the
  name " Hylactor " by " *Ringwood.*" This is clear proof of Shakespeare's indebtedness to Golding in this passage. Actæon's transformation to a horned stag is noticed below, III, ii, 35: " a secure
  and wilful *Actæon.*" The story is told more directly in *Tit. Andr.*,
  II, iii, 61–65, 70–71. Figurative use is made of Actæon's fate in
  Tw. Night, I, i, 22.

I should have borne the humoured letter to her; but I have a sword, and it shall bite upon my necessity. He loves your wife; there's the short and the long. My name is Corporal Nym; I speak, and I avouch; 'tis true: my name is Nym, and Falstaff loves your wife. Adieu. I love not the humour of bread and cheese; and there's the humour of it. Adieu. *[Exit.* 123

PAGE. "The humour of it," quoth 'a! here's a fellow frights English out of his wits.

FORD. I will seek out Falstaff.

PAGE. I never heard such a drawling, affecting rogue.

FORD. If I do find it:— well.

PAGE. I will not believe such a Cataian, though the priest o' the town commended him for a true man. 130

FORD. 'T was a good sensible fellow:— well.

PAGE. How now, Meg!

[Mrs Page and Mrs Ford come forward.

MRS PAGE. Whither go you, George? Hark you.

MRS FORD. How now, sweet Frank! why art thou melancholy?

FORD. I melancholy! I am not melancholy. Get you home, go.

MRS FORD. Faith, thou hast some crotchets in thy head. Now, will you go, Mistress Page? 139

MRS PAGE. Have with you. You'll come to dinner, George? *[Aside to Mrs Ford]* Look who comes yonder: she shall be our messenger to this paltry knight.

---

129 *Cataian*] Literally, a native of Cathay or China, but often used for "thief" or "sharper." Cf. *Tw. Night*, II, iii, 73: "My lady's a *Cataian*."

MRS FORD. [*Aside to Mrs Page*] Trust me, I thought on her: she 'll fit it.

Enter MISTRESS QUICKLY

MRS PAGE. You are come to see my daughter Anne?

QUICK. Ay, forsooth; and, I pray, how does good Mistress Anne?

MRS PAGE. Go in with us and see: we have an hour's talk with you. [*Exeunt Mrs Page, Mrs Ford, and Mrs Quickly.*

PAGE. How now, Master Ford! 150

FORD. You heard what this knave told me, did you not?

PAGE. Yes: and you heard what the other told me?

FORD. Do you think there is truth in them?

PAGE. Hang 'em, slaves! I do not think the knight would offer it: but these that accuse him in his intent towards our wives are a yoke of his discarded men; very rogues, now they be out of service.

FORD. Were they his men?

PAGE. Marry, were they.

FORD. I like it never the better for that. Does he lie at the Garter? 161

PAGE. Ay, marry, does he. If he should intend this voyage toward my wife, I would turn her loose to him; and what he gets more of her than sharp words, let it lie on my head.

FORD. I do not misdoubt my wife; but I would be loath to turn them together. A man may be too confident: I would have nothing lie on my head: I cannot be thus satisfied. 169

[37]

PAGE. Look where my ranting host of the Garter comes: there is either liquor in his pate, or money in his purse, when he looks so merrily.

Enter HOST

How now, mine host!

HOST. How now, bully-rook! thou 'rt a gentleman. Cavaleiro-justice, I say!

Enter SHALLOW

SHAL. I follow, mine host, I follow. Good even and twenty, good Master Page! Master Page, will you go with us? we have sport in hand.

HOST. Tell him, cavaleiro-justice; tell him, bully-rook.

SHAL. Sir, there is a fray to be fought between Sir Hugh the Welsh priest and Caius the French doctor. 181

FORD. Good mine host o' the Garter, a word with you. *[Drawing him aside.*

HOST. What say'st thou, my bully-rook?

SHAL. [*To Page*] Will you go with us to behold it? My merry host hath had the measuring of their weapons; and, I think, hath appointed them contrary places; for, believe me, I hear the parson is no jester. Hark, I will tell you what our sport shall be.

[They converse apart.

HOST. Hast thou no suit against my knight, my guest-cavaleire? 190

FORD. None, I protest: but I'll give you a pottle of burnt sack to give me recourse to him, and tell him my name is Brook; only for a jest.

HOST. My hand, bully; thou shalt have egress and regress;—said I well?—and thy name shall be Brook. It is a merry knight. Will you go, An-heires?

SHAL. Have with you, mine host.

PAGE. I have heard the Frenchman hath good skill in his rapier.   199

SHAL. Tut, sir, I could have told you more. In these times you stand on distance, your passes, stoccadoes, and I know not what: 't is the heart, Master Page; 't is here, 't is here. I have seen the time, with my long sword I would have made you four tall fellows skip like rats.

HOST. Here, boys, here, here! shall we wag?

PAGE. Have with you. I had rather hear them scold than fight.   [*Exeunt Host, Shal., and Page.*   201

FORD. Though Page be a secure fool, and stands so firmly on his wife's frailty, yet I cannot put off my

---

192 *burnt sack*] apparently sack heated by dipping a red-hot iron in the liquid. Cf. *infra*, III, i, 100: "let *burnt sack* be the issue."

196 *An-heires*] This is the reading of the early editions, and is an obvious misprint. Theobald substituted *myn-heers* (*i. e.* the Dutch word for "gentlemen," which was not unfamiliar in colloquial English). It seems more probable that the host used the word "hearts" or "my hearts," *i. e.* brave fellows. This is the host's greeting in like circumstances, III, ii, 75, *infra* ("Farewell, my *hearts*").

208–209 *stands . . . frailty*] Malone explains "has such perfect confidence in his unchaste wife," Ford being supposed to credit every woman with frailty. Theobald read *fealty* for *frailty*, and thus

opinion so easily: she was in his company at Page's house; and what they made there, I know not. Well, I will look further into 't: and I have a disguise to sound Falstaff. If I find her honest, I lose not my labour; if she be otherwise, 't is labour well bestowed.

[*Exit.*

SCENE II—A ROOM IN THE GARTER INN

Enter FALSTAFF *and* PISTOL.

FAL. I will not lend thee a penny.

PIST. Why, then the world 's mine oyster,
Which I with sword will open.

FAL. Not a penny. I have been content, sir, you should lay my countenance to pawn: I have grated upon my good friends for three reprieves for you and your coach-fellow Nym; or else you had looked through the grate, like a geminy of baboons. I am damned in hell for swearing to gentlemen my friends, you were good soldiers and tall fellows; and when Mistress Bridget lost the handle of her fan, I took 't upon mine honour thou 10 hadst it not.

PIST. Didst not thou share? hadst thou not fifteen
pence?

FAL. Reason, you rogue, reason: think'st thou I 'll endanger my soul gratis? At a word, hang no more

removed the ambiguity, which was probably intentional on the author's part.

5–6 *grated upon*] worried, annoyed.

7 *through the grate*] sc. of the prison cell.

about me, I am no gibbet for you. Go. A short
knife and a throng!—To your manor of Pickt-hatch!
Go. You'll not bear a letter for me, you rogue!
you stand upon your honour! Why, thou unconfinable
baseness, it is as much as I can do to keep the terms of
my honour precise: I, I, I myself sometimes, leaving
the fear of God on the left hand, and hiding mine hon- 20
our in my necessity, am fain to shuffle, to hedge, and to
lurch; and yet you, rogue, will ensconce your rags, your
cat-a-mountain looks, your red-lattice phrases, and your
bold-beating oaths, under the shelter of your honour!
You will not do it, you!

PIST. I do relent: what would thou more of man?

Enter ROBIN

ROB. Sir, here's a woman would speak with you.
FAL. Let her approach.

Enter MISTRESS QUICKLY

QUICK. Give your worship good morrow.
FAL. Good morrow, good wife.   30

15–16 *A short knife . . . throng*] Falstaff ironically recommends the
    short knife which cutpurses were wont to turn to account in a
    throng or crowd.
16 *Pickt-hatch*] The name of a street in Clerkenwell, London, which was
    notoriously frequented by loose characters. The name seems to mean
    a hatch (*i. e.* wicket, gate, half door) with pikes or spikes fastened at
    the top. Some of the houses in the street were thus distinguished.
23 *red-lattice phrases*] tavern parlour talk. Cf. *2 Hen. IV*, II, ii, 76:
    "Through a *red-lattice*" *i. e.*, a tavern-window.
24 *bold-beating*] hectoring, braggadocio-like. For this, the original
    reading, Hanmer ingeniously suggested *bull-baiting*.

[41]

QUICK. Not so, an 't please your worship.

FAL. Good maid, then.

QUICK. I 'll be sworn;
As my mother was, the first hour I was born.

FAL. I do believe the swearer. What with me?

QUICK. Shall I vouchsafe your worship a word or two?

FAL. Two thousand, fair woman: and I 'll vouchsafe thee the hearing.

QUICK. There is one Mistress Ford, sir:—I pray, come a little nearer this ways:—I myself dwell with 40 Master Doctor Caius,—

FAL. Well, on: Mistress Ford, you say,—

QUICK. Your worship says very true:—I pray your worship, come a little nearer this ways.

FAL. I warrant thee, nobody hears;—mine own people, mine own people.

QUICK. Are they so? God bless them, and make them his servants!

FAL. Well, Mistress Ford;—what of her?

QUICK. Why, sir, she 's a good creature.—Lord, so Lord! your worship 's a wanton! Well, heaven forgive you and all of us, I pray!

FAL. Mistress Ford;—come, Mistress Ford,—

QUICK. Marry, this is the short and the long of it; you have brought her into such a canaries as 't is wonderful. The best courtier of them all, when the court lay at Windsor, could never have brought her to such a

---

55 *canaries*] a dance with a very quick step. Mrs. Quickly confused the word with "quandary."

canary. Yet there has been knights, and lords, and
gentlemen, with their coaches; I warrant you, coach
after coach, letter after letter, gift after gift; smelling 60
so sweetly, all musk, and so rushling, I warrant you, in
silk and gold; and in such alligant terms; and in such
wine and sugar of the best and the fairest, that would
have won any woman's heart; and, I warrant you, they
could never get an eye-wink of her: I had myself twenty
angels given me this morning; but I defy all angels —
in any such sort, as they say — but in the way of honesty: and, I warrant you, they could never get her so
much as sip on a cup with the proudest of them all: and
yet there has been earls, nay, which is more, pensioners;
but, I warrant you, all is one with her.   70

FAL. But what says she to me? be brief, my good
she-Mercury.

QUICK. Marry, she hath received your letter; for the
which she thanks you a thousand times; and she gives
you to notify, that her husband will be absence from his
house between ten and eleven.

FAL. Ten and eleven.

QUICK. Ay, forsooth; and then you may come and
see the picture, she says, that you wot of: Master Ford,
her husband, will be from home. Alas, the sweet woman 80
leads an ill life with him! he's a very jealousy man: she
leads a very frampold life with him, good heart.

FEL. Ten and eleven. Woman, commend me to her;
I will not fail her.

---

69 *pensioners*] gentlemen of the sovereign's body guard.

QUICK. Why, you say well. But I have another messenger to your worship. Mistress Page hath her hearty commendations to you, too : and let me tell you in your ear, she's as fartuous a civil modest wife, and one, I tell you, that will not miss you morning nor evening prayer, as any is in Windsor, whoe'er be the other : and she bade 90 me tell your worship that her husband is seldom from home ; but, she hopes, there will come a time. I never knew a woman so dote upon a man : surely, I think you have charms, la ; yes, in truth.

FAL. Not I, I assure thee : setting the attraction of my good parts aside, I have no other charms.

QUICK. Blessing on your heart for 't !

FAL. But, I pray thee, tell me this : has Ford's wife and Page's wife acquainted each other how they love me ? 98

QUICK. That were a jest indeed ! they have not so little grace, I hope : that were a trick indeed ! But Mistress Page would desire you to send her your little page, of all loves : her husband has a marvellous infection to the little page ; and, truly, Master Page is an honest man. Never a wife in Windsor leads a better life than she does : do what she will, say what she will, take all, pay all, go to bed when she list, rise when she list, all is as she will : and, truly, she deserves it ; for if there be a kind woman in Windsor, she is one. You must send her your page ; no remedy. 110

---

103 *of all loves*] In *Othello*, III, i, 13, the Quarto reading, " Desire you *of all loves*," is altered in the Folios to *for loves sake*, the obvious meaning of the very common expression.

FAL. Why, I will.

QUICK. Nay, but do so, then: and, look you, he may come and go between you both; and, in any case, have a nay-word, that you may know one another's mind, and the boy never need to understand any thing; for 't is not good that children should know any wickedness: old folks, you know, have discretion, as they say, and know the world.

FAL. Fare thee well: commend me to them both: there's my purse; I am yet thy debtor. Boy, go along with this woman. [*Exeunt Mistress Quickly and Robin.*] This news distracts me! 121

PIST. This punk is one of Cupid's carriers:
Clap on more sails; pursue; up with your fights:
Give fire: she is my prize, or ocean whelm them all!

[*Exit.*

FAL. Say'st thou so, old Jack? go thy ways; I 'll make more of thy old body than I have done. Will they yet look after thee? Wilt thou, after the expense of so much money, be now a gainer? Good body, I thank thee. Let them say 't is grossly done; so it be fairly done, no matter.

Enter BARDOLPH

BARD. Sir John, there's one Master Brook below would fain speak with you, and be acquainted with

114 *nay-word*] Cf. V, ii, 5, *infra*, "We have a *nay-word* (*i. e.* pass word) how to know one another."
123 *fights*] "fighting sails," or screens which were hung round the decks of ships in action; a technical term in nautical treatises.

you; and hath sent your worship a morning's draught of sack. 139

FAL. Brook is his name?

BARD. Ay, sir.

FAL. Call him in. [*Exit Bardolph.*] Such Brooks are welcome to me, that o'erflow such liquor. Ah, ha! Mistress Ford and Mistress Page, have I encompassed you? go to; via!

Re-enter BARDOLPH, *with* FORD *disguised*

FORD. Bless you, sir!

FAL. And you, sir! Would you speak with me?

FORD. I make bold to press with so little preparation upon you. 141

FAL. You 're welcome. What 's your will? — Give us leave, drawer. [*Exit Bardolph.*

FORD. Sir, I am a gentleman that have spent much; my name is Brook.

FAL. Good Master Brook, I desire more acquaintance of you.

FORD. Good Sir John, I sue for yours: not to charge you; for I must let you understand I think myself in better plight for a lender than you are: the which hath something emboldened me to this unseasoned intrusion; for they say, if money go before, all ways do lie open. 152

FAL. Money is a good soldier, sir, and will on.

FORD. Troth, and I have a bag of money here troubles me: if you will help to bear it, Sir John, take all, or half, for easing me of the carriage.

[46]

FAL. Sir, I know not how I may deserve to be your porter.

FORD. I will tell you, sir, if you will give me the hearing.

FAL. Speak, good Master Brook: I shall be glad to be your servant. 161

FORD. Sir, I hear you are a scholar, — I will be brief with you, — and you have been a man long known to me, though I had never so good means, as desire, to make myself acquainted with you. I shall discover a thing to you, wherein I must very much lay open mine own imperfection: but, good Sir John, as you have one eye upon my follies, as you hear them unfolded, turn another into the register of your own; that I may pass with a reproof the easier, sith you yourself know how easy it is to be such an offender. 170

FAL. Very well, sir; proceed.

FORD. There is a gentlewoman in this town; her husband's name is Ford.

FAL. Well, sir.

FORD. I have long loved her, and, I protest to you, bestowed much on her; followed her with a doting observance; engrossed opportunities to meet her; fee'd every slight occasion that could but niggardly give me sight of her; not only bought many presents to give her, but have given largely to many to know what she would have given; briefly, I have pursued her as love hath pursued me; which hath been on the wing of all occasions. But whatsoever I have merited, either in my mind or in my means, meed, I am sure, I have received none; un-

[47]

less experience be a jewel that I have purchased at an
infinite rate, and that hath taught me to say this:

> "Love like a shadow flies when substance love pursues;
> Pursuing that that flies, and flying what pursues."

FAL. Have you received no promise of satisfaction at
her hands?   190

FORD. Never.

FAL. Have you importuned her to such a purpose?

FORD. Never.

FAL. Of what quality was your love, then?

FORD. Like a fair house built on another man's
ground; so that I have lost my edifice by mistaking
the place where I erected it.   197

FAL. To what purpose have you unfolded this to me?

FORD. When I have told you that, I have told you
all. Some say, that though she appear honest to me,
yet in other places she enlargeth her mirth so far that
there is shrewd construction made of her. Now, Sir
John, here is the heart of my purpose: you are a
gentleman of excellent breeding, admirable discourse,
of great admittance, authentic in your place and person,
generally allowed for your many war-like, court-like, and
learned preparations.

FAL. O, sir!

FORD. Believe it, for you know it. There is money;

204–205 *of great admittance . . . allowed*] being admitted into or fitted
for great society, holding a position of recognized authority and
importance, and being generally allowed or commended, etc. Cf.
"of Venetian *admittance*," III, iii, 49, *infra.*

spend it, spend it ; spend more ; spend all I have ; only
give me so much of your time in exchange of it, as to lay
an amiable siege to the honesty of this Ford's wife : use
your art of wooing ; win her to consent to you : if any
man may, you may as soon as any.   213

FAL. Would it apply well to the vehemency of your
affection, that I should win what you would enjoy ? Methinks you prescribe to yourself very preposterously.

FORD. O, understand my drift. She dwells so securely
on the excellency of her honour, that the folly of my soul
dares not present itself : she is too bright to be looked
against. Now, could I come to her with any detection
in my hand, my desires had instance and argument to
commend themselves : I could drive her then from the
ward of her purity, her reputation, her marriage-vow,
and a thousand other her defences, which now are too
too strongly embattled against me. What say you to 't,
Sir John ?   225

FAL. Master Brook, I will first make bold with your
money ; next, give me your hand ; and last, as I am a
gentleman, you shall, if you will, enjoy Ford's wife.

FORD. O good sir !

FAL. I say you shall.   230

FORD. Want no money, Sir John ; you shall want
none.

FAL. Want no Mistress Ford, Master Brook ; you
shall want none. I shall be with her, I may tell you,
by her own appointment ; even as you came in to me,
her assistant, or go-between, parted from me : I say I
shall be with her between ten and eleven ; for at that

time the jealous rascally knave her husband will be
forth. Come you to me at night; you shall know how
I speed.

FORD. I am blest in your acquaintance. Do you
know Ford, sir? 240

FAL. Hang him, poor cuckoldly knave! I know him
not:—yet I wrong him to call him poor; they say the
jealous wittolly knave hath masses of money; for the
which his wife seems to me well-favoured. I will use
her as the key of the cuckoldly rogue's coffer; and
there's my harvest-home.

FORD. I would you knew Ford, sir, that you might
avoid him, if you saw him. 247

FAL. Hang him, mechanical salt-butter rogue! I
will stare him out of his wits; I will awe him with my
cudgel: it shall hang like a meteor o'er the cuckold's
horns. Master Brook, thou shalt know I will predomi-
nate over the peasant, and thou shalt lie with his wife.
Come to me soon at night. Ford's a knave, and I will
aggravate his style; thou, Master Brook, shalt know
him for knave and cuckold. Come to me soon at
night. [Exit. 255

FORD. What a damned Epicurean rascal is this!
My heart is ready to crack with impatience. Who says

248 *mechanical salt-butter rogue*] an artisan, who never tasted anything
but salt butter. Cf. Fletcher's *Maid in the Mill*, III, 2, where it
is abusively said of a tailor, "Let him call at home in's own house
for *salt-butter*."

253 *aggravate his style*] add more titles (*i. e.* "knave" and "cuckold")
to those he already enjoys.

this is improvident jealously? my wife hath sent to him; the hour is fixed; the match is made. Would any man have thought this? See the hell of having a false woman! My bed shall be abused, my coffers ransacked, my reputation gnawn at; and I shall not only receive this villanous wrong, but stand under the adoption of abominable terms, and by him that does me this wrong. Terms! names!— Amaimon sounds well; Lucifer, well; Barbason, well; yet they are devils' additions, the names of fiends: but Cuckold! Wittol! — Cuckold! the devil himself hath not such a name. Page is an ass, a secure ass: he will trust his wife; he will not be jealous. I will rather trust a Fleming with my butter, Parson Hugh the Welshman with my cheese, an Irishman with my aqua-vitæ bottle, or a thief to walk my ambling gelding, than my wife with herself: then she plots, then she ruminates, then she devises; and what they think in their hearts they may effect, they will break their hearts but they will effect. God be praised for my jealousy!— Eleven o'clock the hour. I will prevent this, detect my wife, be revenged on Falstaff, and laugh at Page. I will about it; better three hours too soon than a minute too late. Fie, fie, fie! cuckold! cuckold! cuckold!   [*Exit.* 279

---

264 *Amaimon*] The name of a demon or sprite, which figures in Reginald Scot's *Discovery of Witchcraft*, Bk. XV, ch. ii.

265 *Barbason*] represents Scot's fiend of hell called "Barbatos." Nym mentions him again in *Hen. V*, II, i, 52: "I am not *Barbason*."

271 *aqua-vitæ*] Usquebaugh, strong spirits, with indulgence in which Irishmen were commonly credited.

SCENE III — A FIELD NEAR WINDSOR

Enter CAIUS *and* RUGBY

CAIUS. Jack Rugby!

RUG. Sir?

CAIUS. Vat is de clock, Jack?

RUG. 'T is past the hour, sir, that Sir Hugh promised
to meet.

CAIUS. By gar, he has save his soul, dat he is no
come; he has pray his Pible well, dat he is no come:
by gar, Jack Rugby, he is dead already, if he be come.

RUG. He is wise, sir; he knew your worship would
kill him, if he came.   10

CAIUS. By gar, de herring is no dead so as I vill kill
him.   Take your rapier, Jack; I vill tell you how I vill
kill him.

RUG. Alas, sir, I cannot fence.

CAIUS. Villainy, take your rapier.

RUG. Forbear; here's company.

Enter HOST, SHALLOW, SLENDER, *and* PAGE

HOST. Bless thee, bully doctor!

SHAL. Save you, Master Doctor Gaius!

PAGE. Now, good master doctor!

SLEN. Give you good morrow, sir.   20

CAIUS. Vat be all you, one, two, tree, four, come for?

HOST. To see thee fight, to see thee foin, to see thee

22-25 *to see* . . . *montant*] Mine Host rattles off a long series of fencing
terms. Thus " foin " is to " thrust "; " traverse " is to " parry ";

[52]

traverse; to see thee here, to see thee there; to see thee
pass thy punto, thy stock, thy reverse, thy distance, thy
montant. Is he dead, my Ethiopian? is he dead, my
Francisco? ha, bully! What says my Æsculapius? my
Galen? my heart of elder? ha! is he dead, bully-stale?
is he dead?

CAIUS. By gar, he is de coward Jack priest of de
vorld; he is not show his face.

HOST. Thou art a Castalion-King-Urinal. Hector of
Greece, my boy!

CAIUS. I pray you, bear vitness that me have stay six
or seven, two, tree hours for him, and he is no come.

SHAL. He is the wiser man, master doctor: he is a
curer of souls, and you a curer of bodies; if you should
fight, you go against the hair of your professions. Is it
not true, Master Page?

PAGE. Master Shallow, you have yourself been a
great fighter, though now a man of peace.

"punto" and "stock" i. e. stoccato, both mean "thrust"; "reverse" is a backhanded stroke; "distance" is the space between
the antagonists; "montant," or "montanto," is a direct blow.
27 *my heart of elder*] a burlesque parody of "heart of oak"; the
elder-tree's heart is of pith.
30 *Castalion-King-Urinal*] This is the reading of the Folios. But the
meaning is improved by the commonly accepted change, *Castilian,
King-urinal!* "Castilian" was an epithet commonly applied to
a braggadocio. In vulgar talk Elizabethan doctors were often
jeered at for their professional practice of inspecting urine. The
like intention is apparent in the host's insolent exclamations
"bully-stale" (l. 27) and "Mock water" i. e. "Muck-water"
(l. 51).

[53]

SHAL. Bodykins, Master Page, though I now be old, 40
and of the peace, if I see a sword out, my finger itches
to make one. Though we are justices, and doctors,
and churchmen, Master Page, we have some salt of our
youth in us ; we are the sons of women, Master Page.

PAGE. 'T is true, Master Shallow.

SHAL. It will be found so, Master Page. Master
Doctor Caius, I am come to fetch you home. I am
sworn of the peace : you have shewed yourself a wise
physician, and Sir Hugh hath shewn himself a wise and
patient churchman. You must go with me, master
doctor. 50

HOST. Pardon, guest-justice. — A word, Mounseur
Mock-water.

CAIUS. Mock-vater ! vat is dat ?

HOST. Mock-water, in our English tongue, is valour,
bully.

CAIUS. By gar, den, I have as much mock-vater as de
Englishman. — Scurvy jack-dog priest ! by gar, me vill
cut his ears.

HOST. He will clapper-claw thee tightly, bully.

CAIUS. Clapper-de-claw ! vat is dat ? 60

HOST. That is, he will make thee amends.

CAIUS. By gar, me do look he shall clapper-de-claw
me ; for, by gar, me vill have it.

HOST. And I will provoke him to 't, or let him wag.

CAIUS. Me tank you for dat.

HOST. And, moreover, bully, — But first, master

---

51 *Mock-water*] See note on l. 30, *supra*.

guest, and Master Page, and eke Cavaleiro Slender, go you through the town to Frogmore. [*Aside to them.*

PAGE. Sir Hugh is there, is he?

HOST. He is there : see what humour he is in; and I 70 will bring the doctor about by the fields. Will it do well?

SHAL. We will do it.

PAGE, SHAL., and SLEN. Adieu, good master doctor.
[Exeunt Page, Shal., and Slen.

CAIUS. By gar, me vill kill de priest ; for he speak for a jack-an-ape to Anne Page.

HOST. Let him die : sheathe thy impatience, throw cold water on thy choler : go about the fields with me through Frogmore : I will bring thee where Mistress Anne Page is, at a farm-house a-feasting ; and thou 80 shalt woo her. Cried I aim? said I well?

CAIUS. By gar, me dank you vor dat : by gar, I love you ; and I shall procure-a you de good guest, de earl, de knight, de lords, de gentlemen, my patients.

HOST. For the which I will be thy adversary toward Anne Page. Said I well?

CAIUS. By gar, 't is good ; vell said.

HOST. Let us wag, then.

CAIUS. Come at my heels, Jack Rugby. [*Exeunt.*

---

81 *Cried I aim?*] This is Douce's ingenious emendation for the Folio reading *Cride-game.* The earlier Quartos read *cried game.* "To cry aim," *i. e.* to stand beside the archer and to suggest the direction of his aim, is a technical phrase in archery. The host asks if he has not given the doctor good advice in his suit. "Cry aim" is used in a cognate sense, III, ii, 37, *infra,* "all my neighbours shall *cry aim* (*i. e.* give encouragement).

ACT THIRD — SCENE I
A FIELD NEAR FROGMORE
Enter SIR HUGH EVANS *and* SIMPLE

EVANS

PRAY YOU NOW, GOOD Master Slender's serving-man, and friend Simple by your name, which way have you looked for Master Caius, that calls himself doctor of physic ?

SIM. Marry, sir, the pittie-ward, the park-ward, every way ; old Windsor way, and every way but the town way.

EVANS. I most fehemently desire you you will also look that way.

SIM. I will, sir.　　　　　　[*Exit.*

EVANS. Pless my soul, how full of chollors I am, and 10 trempling of mind ! — I shall be glad if he have deceived me. — How melancholies I am ! — I will knog his urinals

[56]

about his knave's costard when I have goot opportunities
for the ork. — Pless my soul ! —   [*Sings.*

> To shallow rivers, to whose falls
> Melodious birds sings madrigals ;
> There will we make our peds of roses,
> And a thousand fragrant posies.
> To shallow —

Mercy on me ! I have a great dispositions to cry. [*Sings.* 20

> Melodious birds sing madrigals —
> Whenas I sat in Pabylon —

---

5 *pittie-ward*] This word, which is altered in the second and later Folios
to *pitty-wary*, has not been satisfactorily explained. The early
emendation *city-ward* circumvents the difficulty. The suggestion
that the word is equivalent to " pitwards," towards the pit, *i. e.* a
sawpit or gravel pit (in or about Windsor), is speciously supported
by the mention of " a sawpit," *infra*, IV, iv, 52 ; of " a pit hard by
Herne's oak," V, iii, 13 ; and of " the pit," V, iv, 2. From the
fact that medieval Bristol was credited by William of Worcester
with a street called " Via de Pyttey," and with a gate called
" Pyttey Gate," it may be that a like name was applied to some
thoroughfare of Elizabethan Windsor.

15 *To shallow rivers, etc.*] These four lines form part of the lyric " Come
live with me and be my love " (assigned to Christopher Marlowe),
which was first printed in Jaggard's piratical miscellany called
" *The Passionate Pilgrime*, By W. Shakespeare, 1599." See *The
Passionate Pilgrim* facsimile (Oxford, 1905, Preface, pp. 35–38).

22 *Whenas I sat in Pabylon*] This is an interpolation into Marlowe's
poem. Sir Hugh in his confusion jumbles his quotations. There
is doubtless a reminiscence of *Ps.* cxxxvii, 1 : " By the waters
of Babylon we sat down and wept." But it should be noted that
in the First (imperfect) Quarto of the play (1602) Evans prefixes
to his repetition of Marlowe's lines the words (omitted in the
Folio), " There dwelt a man in Babylon." That is the first line

And a thousand vagram posies.
To shallow &c.

Re-enter SIMPLE

SIM. Yonder he is coming, this way, Sir Hugh.
EVANS. He's welcome. —   [*Sings.*

To shallow rivers, to whose falls —

Heaven prosper the right ! — What weapons is he ?
SIM. No weapons, sir. There comes my master,
Master Shallow, and another gentleman, from Frog- 30
more, over the style, this way.
EVANS. Pray you, give me my gown ; or else keep it
in your arms.

Enter PAGE, SHALLOW, *and* SLENDER

SHAL. How now, master parson ! Good morrow,
good Sir Hugh. Keep a gamester from the dice, and
a good student from his book, and it is wonderful.
SLEN. [*Aside*] Ah, sweet Anne Page !
PAGE. Save you, good Sir Hugh !
EVANS. Pless you from his mercy sake, all of you !
SHAL. What, the sword and the word ! do you study 40
them both, master parson ?
PAGE. And youthful still ! in your doublet and hose
this raw rheumatic day !
EVANS. There is reasons and causes for it.

---

of another popular contemporary ballad known as *The Ballad of
Constant Susanna ;* the same line is quoted by Sir Toby Belch in
Tw. Night, II, iii, 76.

[58]

PAGE. We are come to you to do a good office, master parson.

EVANS. Fery well: what is it?

PAGE. Yonder is a most reverend gentleman, who, belike having received wrong by some person, is at most odds with his own gravity and patience that ever you saw.

SHAL. I have lived fourscore years and upward; I never heard a man of his place, gravity, and learning, so wide of his own respect.

EVANS. What is he?

PAGE. I think you know him; Master Doctor Caius, the renowned French physician.

EVANS. Got's will, and his passion of my heart! I had as lief you would tell me of a mess of porridge.

PAGE. Why?

EVANS. He has no more knowledge in Hibocrates and Galen, — and he is a knave besides; a cowardly knave as you would desires to be acquainted withal.

PAGE. I warrant you, he's the man should fight with him.

SLEN. [*Aside*] O sweet Anne Page!

SHAL. It appears so, by his weapons. Keep them asunder: here comes Doctor Caius.

Enter HOST, CAIUS, *and* RUGBY

PAGE. Nay, good master parson, keep in your weapon.

SHAL. So do you, good master doctor.

HOST. Disarm them, and let them question: let them 70
keep their limbs whole, and hack our English.

CAIUS. I pray you, let-a me speak a word with your
ear. Verefore vill you not meet-a me?

EVANS. [*Aside to Caius*] Pray you, use your patience:
in good time.

CAIUS. By gar, you are de coward, de Jack dog,
John ape.

EVANS. [*Aside to Caius*] Pray you, let us not be laugh-
ing-stocks to other men's humours; I desire you in
friendship, and I will one way or other make you 80
amends. [*Aloud*] I will knog your urinals about your
knave's cogscomb for missing your meetings and
appointments.

CAIUS. Diable!—Jack Rugby,—mine host de Jarteer,—have I not stay for him to kill him? have I not,
at de place I did appoint?

EVANS. As I am a Christians soul, now, look you,
this is the place appointed: I'll be judgement by mine
host of the Garter.

HOST. Peace, I say, Gallia and Gaul, French and
Welsh, soul-curer and body-curer!   90

CAIUS. Ay, dat is very good; excellent.

HOST. Peace, I say! hear mine host of the Garter.
Am I politic? am I subtle? am I a Machiavel? Shall
I lose my doctor? no; he gives me the potions and the
motions. Shall I lose my parson, my priest, my Sir
Hugh? no; he gives me the proverbs and the no-verbs.
Give me thy hand, terrestrial; so. Give me thy hand,
celestial; so. Boys of art, I have deceived you both; I

have directed you to wrong places : your hearts are mighty, your skins are whole, and let burnt sack be the issue. Come, lay their swords to pawn. Follow me, lads of peace ; follow, follow, follow.   108

SHAL. Trust me, a mad host. Follow, gentlemen, follow.

SLEN. [*Aside*] O sweet Anne Page !

[*Exeunt Shal., Slen., Page, and Host.*

CAIUS. Ha, do I perceive dat ? have you make-a de sot of us, ha, ha ?

EVANS. This is well ; he has made us his vlouting-stog. — I desire you that we may be friends ; and let us knog our prains together to be revenge on this same scall, scurvy, cogging companion, the host of the Garter.   111

CAIUS. By gar, with all my heart. He promise to bring me where is Anne Page ; by gar, he deceive me too.

EVANS. Well, I will smite his noddles. Pray you, follow.   [*Exeunt.*

SCENE II—THE STREET, IN WINDSOR

Enter MISTRESS PAGE *and* ROBIN

MRS PAGE. Nay, keep your way, little gallant ; you were wont to be a follower, but now you are a leader.

---

100 *burnt sack*] See II, i, 192, *supra*.

108 *vlouting-stog*] Evans' mispronunciation of "flouting-stock," *i. e.* butt. Cf. IV, v, 74, *infra*.

110 *scall*] "Scall" is equivalent to "scald," and means much the same as "scurvy," the word which follows.

Whether had you rather lead mine eyes, or eye your master's heels?

Rob. I had rather, forsooth, go before you like a man than follow him like a dwarf.

Mrs Page. O, you are a flattering boy: now I see you 'll be a courtier.

Enter Ford

Ford. Well met, Mistress Page. Whither go you?

Mrs Page. Truly, sir, to see your. wife. Is she at home?

Ford. Ay; and as idle as she may hang together, for 10 want of company. I think, if your husbands were dead, you two would marry.

Mrs Page. Be sure of that, — two other husbands.

Ford. Where had you this pretty weathercock?

Mrs Page. I cannot tell what the dickens his name is my husband had him of. — What do you call your knight's name, sirrah?

Rob. Sir John Falstaff.

Ford. Sir John Falstaff!

Mrs Page. He, he; I can never hit on 's name. 20 There is such a league between my good man and he! — Is your wife at home indeed?

Ford. Indeed she is.

---

10 *as idle as she may hang together*] as idle as one can possibly be: a colloquialism equivalent to the modern slang "as idle as she can stick."

MRS PAGE. By your leave, sir : I am sick till I see
her.   [*Exeunt Mrs Page and Robin.*

FORD. Has Page any brains ? hath he any eyes ? hath
he any thinking ? Sure, they sleep ; he hath no use of
them. Why, this boy will carry a letter twenty mile,
as easy as a cannon will shoot point-blank twelve score.
He pieces out his wife's inclination ; he gives her folly
motion and advantage : and now she 's going to my 30
wife, and Falstaff's boy with her. A man may hear
this shower sing in the wind. And Falstaff's boy
with her ! Good plots, they are laid ; and our re-
volted wives share damnation together. Well ; I will
take him, then torture my wife, pluck the borrowed veil
of modesty from the so seeming Mistress Page, divulge
Page himself for a secure and wilful Actæon ; and to
these violent proceedings all my neighbours shall cry aim.
[*Clock heard.*]   The clock gives me my cue, and my assurance bids me search : there I shall find Falstaff: I shall
be rather praised for this than mocked ; for it is as 40
positive as the earth is firm that Falstaff is there: I
will go.

---

28 *twelve score*] twelve score yards.

31-32 *may hear this shower . . . wind*] A phrase implying the coming
   of a storm, which is often heralded by a whistling or singing note
   in the rising wind. Cf. *Tempest*, II, ii, 19 : " Another storm brew-
   ing : I hear it *sing i' the wind*."

36 *Actæon*] For another reference to this mythical hero see *supra*, II,
   i, 106.

37 *cry aim*] give encouragement. See *supra*, II, iii, 81 and note,
   " Cried I aim ? "

Enter PAGE, SHALLOW, SLENDER, Host, SIR HUGH EVANS, CAIUS, *and* RUGBY

SHAL., PAGE, &c. Well met, Master Ford.

FORD. Trust me, a good knot: I have good cheer at home; and I pray you all go with me.

SHAL. I must excuse myself, Master Ford.

SLEN. And so must I, sir: we have appointed to dine with Mistress Anne, and I would not break with her for more money than I'll speak of.

SHAL. We have lingered about a match between Anne Page and my cousin Slender, and this day we so shall have our answer.

SLEN. I hope I have your good will, father Page.

PAGE. You have, Master Slender; I stand wholly for you: — but my wife, master doctor, is for you altogether.

CAIUS. Ay, be-gar; and de maid is love-a me: my nursh-a Quickly tell me so mush.

HOST. What say you to young Master Fenton? he capers, he dances, he has eyes of youth, he writes verses, he speaks holiday, he smells April and May: he will carry 't, he will carry 't; 'tis in his buttons; he will so carry 't.

---

43 *a good knot*] a welcome gathering of friends. Cf. IV, ii, 103: "A *knot, a ging, a pack.*"

59 *speaks holiday*] uses choice phrases. Cf. "High-day writ," *Merch. of Ven.*, II, ix, 98, and "festival terms," *Much Ado*, V, ii, 37.

60 *in his buttons*] altogether in his compass or ability. Cf. Marston, *The Fawn*, II, i, 66: "Thou art now *within the buttons* of the prince," *i. e.*, in the innermost confidence of the prince.

PAGE. Not by my consent, I promise you. The gentleman is of no having: he kept company with the wild prince and Poins; he is of too high a region; he knows too much. No, he shall not knit a knot in his fortunes with the finger of my substance: if he take her, let him take her simply; the wealth I have waits on my consent, and my consent goes not that way.

FORD. I beseech you heartily, some of you go home with me to dinner: besides your cheer, you shall have sport; I will show you a monster. Master doctor, you 70 shall go; so shall you, Master Page; and you, Sir Hugh.

SHAL. Well, fare you well: we shall have the freer wooing at Master Page's. [*Exeunt Shal. and Slen.*

CAIUS. Go home, John Rugby; I come anon.

[*Exit Rugby.*

HOST. Farewell, my hearts: I will to my honest knight Falstaff, and drink canary with him. [*Exit.*

FORD. [*Aside*] I think I shall drink in pipe-wine first

---

62 *no having*] no property or fortune. Cf. *Tw. Night*, III, iv, 329: "my *having* is not much."

63 *the wild prince and Poins*] Prince Hal, afterwards Henry V, and his favourite companion Poins, both of whom are leading characters in the two parts of *Hen. IV*.

   too high a region] too high a rank, too highly placed. "Region" is often applied to the highest layers of the atmospheric air.

77 *drink in pipe-wine*] There is a pun on the word "pipe," which is employed in the double sense of an instrument used for dance-music and a liquid-measure. Similarly, "canary" is both a dance and a wine. The meaning is to the same effect as that of the next sentence: "I'll make him dance." "Drink in" is equivalent to "drink." "Pipe-wine" is literally wine drawn from the pipe (or barrel of two hogsheads).

5 [65]

with him; I'll make him dance. Will you go,
gentles?

ALL. Have with you to see this monster. [*Exeunt.*

SCENE III — A ROOM IN FORD'S HOUSE

Enter MISTRESS FORD *and* MISTRESS PAGE

MRS FORD. What, John! What, Robert!
MRS PAGE. Quickly, quickly!—is the buck-basket—
MRS FORD. I warrant. What, Robin, I say!

Enter Servants *with a basket*

MRS PAGE. Come, come, come.
MRS FORD. Here, set it down.
MRS PAGE. Give your men the charge; we must be
brief.
MRS FORD. Marry, as I told you before, John and
Robert, be ready here hard by in the brew-house; and
when I suddenly call you, come forth, and, without any
pause or staggering, take this basket on your shoulders : 10
that done, trudge with it in all haste, and carry it among
the whitsters in Datchet-mead, and there empty it in
the muddy ditch close by the Thames side.
MRS PAGE. You will do it?

2 *buck-basket*] The basket in which dirty clothes were sent to be
" bucked," or washed by the thorough process commonly known
as " bucking." Much play is made of the word buck, *infra*,
lines 237–239.

MRS FORD. I ha' told them over and over; they lack no direction. Be gone, and come when you are called.

[Exeunt Servants.

MRS PAGE. Here comes little Robin.

Enter ROBIN

MRS FORD. How now, my eyas-musket ! what news with you ?

ROB. My master, Sir John, is come in at your back- 20 door, Mistress Ford, and requests your company.

MRS PAGE. You little Jack-a-Lent, have you been true to us ?

ROB. Ay, I 'll be sworn. My master knows not of your being here, and hath threatened to put me into everlasting liberty, if I tell you of it ; for he swears he 'll turn me away.

MRS PAGE. Thou 'rt a good boy : this secrecy of thine shall be a tailor to thee, and shall make thee a new doublet and hose. I 'll go hide me.

MRS FORD. Do so. Go tell thy master I am alone. 30 [*Exit Robin.*] Mistress Page, remember you your cue.

MRS PAGE. I warrant thee ; if I do not act it, hiss me. [*Exit.*

MRS FORD. Go to, then : we 'll use this unwholesome

---

22 *Jack-a-Lent*] a puppet, at which, during Lent, children at play flung sticks or stones. The word is repeated *infra*, V, v, 123. Cf. *Greenes Tu Quoque* (1614): "if a boy that in throwing at his *Jack-a-Lent* chance to hit me on the shins " (Dodsley's *Old Plays*, ed. Hazlitt, XI, 262).

humidity, this gross watery pumpion ; we 'll teach him
to know turtles from jays.

Enter FALSTAFF

FAL. " Have I caught " thee, " my heavenly jewel ? "
Why, now let me die, for I have lived long enough : this
is the period of my ambition : O this blessed hour !

MRS FORD. O sweet Sir John !

FAL. Mistress Ford, I cannot cog, I cannot prate, 40
Mistress Ford. Now shall I sin in my wish : I would
thy husband were dead : I 'll speak it before the best
lord ; I would make thee my lady.

MRS FORD. I your lady, Sir John ! alas, I should be
a pitiful lady !

FAL. Let the court of France show me such another.
I see how thine eye would emulate the diamond : thou
hast the right arched beauty of the brow that becomes
the ship-tire, the tire-valiant, or any tire of Venetian
admittance.

---

35 *turtles from jays*] faithful wives from loose women. Cf. *Cymb.*, III,
   iv, 52 : " Some *jay* of Italy." In Italian *putta* means both jay and
   harlot.

36 *" Have I caught "* . . . *" my heavenly jewel ? "*] These words form
   the first line of the second song in Sir Philip Sidney's *Astrophel
   and Stella* (first published in 1591). The early Quartos of the
   play rightly omit *thee.*

48-49 *the ship-tire* . . . *of Venetian admittance*] Falstaff refers to three
   kinds of headdress, firstly that shaped like a ship, secondly " the
   tire-valiant," and lastly that of the quality held in esteem at
   Venice, in the Venetian fashion. (Cf. *" of great admittance,"* II, ii,
   204, *supra.*) The " tire-valiant " is not easy to explain. The early

MRS FORD. A plain kerchief, Sir John: my brows 50
become nothing else; nor that well neither.

FAL. By the Lord, thou art a traitor to say so: thou
wouldst make an absolute courtier; and the firm fixture
of thy foot would give an excellent motion to thy gait
in a semi-circled farthingale. I see what thou wert, if
Fortune thy foe were not, Nature thy friend. Come,
thou canst not hide it.

MRS FORD. Believe me, there's no such thing in me.

FAL. What made me love thee? let that persuade
thee there's something extraordinary in thee. Come,
I cannot cog, and say thou art this and that, like a 60
many of these lisping hawthorn-buds, that come like
women in men's apparel, and smell like Bucklersbury
in simple time; I cannot: but I love thee; none but
thee; and thou deservest it.

MRS FORD. Do not betray me, sir. I fear you love
Mistress Page.

Quartos read "tire-vellet" (i. e. velvet), which makes good sense.
Stubbes in his *Anatomie of Abuses*, Vol. I, p. 69, denounces with
heat velvet ornaments for the head. "Tire-valiant" can only
mean headdress of very "brave" i. e. showy, design.

55 *Fortune thy foe*] "Fortune my foe" are the opening words of a popular ballad deploring the caprices of Fortune. It is found in early
ballad collections, and runs to twenty-two stanzas. The opening
line runs, "*Fortune my foe*, why dost thou frown on me?" Cf.
"*Fortune my foe* is a friend to it" (Beaumont and Fletcher's
Custom of the Country, I, i, 13). The whole of the first stanza is
quoted in the comedy, *The Maydes Metamorphosis*, 1600.

62 *Bucklersbury*] A street at the east end of Cheapside, London, which
was full of apothecaries' shops and was redolent of medicinal herbs
or simples in early summer, when they were freshly stored.

FAL. Thou mightst as well say I love to walk by the Counter-gate, which is as hateful to me as the reek of a lime-kiln.

MRS FORD. Well, heaven knows how I love you; and you shall one day find it.   70

FAL. Keep in that mind; I 'll deserve it.

MRS FORD. Nay, I must tell you, so you do; or else I could not be in that mind.

ROB. [*Within*] Mistress Ford, Mistress Ford! here 's Mistress Page at the door, sweating, and blowing, and looking wildly, and would needs speak with you presently.

FAL. She shall not see me: I will ensconce me behind the arras.

MRS FORD. Pray you, do so: she 's a very tattling woman.   [*Falstaff hides himself.* 80

Re-enter MISTRESS PAGE *and* ROBIN

What 's the matter? how now!

MRS PAGE. O Mistress Ford, what have you done? You 're shamed, you 're overthrown, you 're undone for ever!

---

67 *Counter-gate*] the gate of the gaol. Two prisons in the city of London were known respectively as the Wood Street *Counter*, the Poultry *Counter*. "The *Counter*" was the title of the gaol in Southwark.

78 *the arras*] the tapestry which hung from wooden rods at a little distance from the wall of the room. Falstaff, in *1 Hen. IV*, II, iv, Borachio in *Much Ado*, I, iii, and Polonius in *Hamlet*, III, iii, all seek the same hiding-place.

MRS FORD. What's the matter, good Mistress Page?

MRS PAGE. O well-a-day, Mistress Ford! having an honest man to your husband, to give him such cause of suspicion!

MRS FORD. What cause of suspicion?

MRS PAGE. What cause of suspicion! Out upon you! how am I mistook in you!   90

MRS FORD. Why, alas, what's the matter?

MRS PAGE. Your husband's coming hither, woman, with all the officers in Windsor, to search for a gentleman that he says is here now in the house, by your consent, to take an ill advantage of his absence: you are undone.

MRS FORD. 'T is not so, I hope.

MRS PAGE. Pray heaven it be not so, that you have such a man here! but 't is most certain your husband's coming, with half Windsor at his heels, to search for such a one. I come before to tell you. If you know yourself clear, why, I am glad of it; but if you have a friend here, convey, convey him out. Be not amazed; call all your senses to you; defend your reputation, or bid farewell to your good life for ever.   100

MRS FORD. What shall I do? There is a gentleman my dear friend; and I fear not mine own shame so much as his peril: I had rather than a thousand pound he were out of the house.

MRS PAGE. For shame! never stand "you had rather" and "you had rather:" your husband's here at hand; bethink you of some conveyance: in the house you

[71]

cannot hide him. O, how have you deceived me! Look, here is a basket: if he be of any reasonable stature, he may creep in here; and throw foul linen upon him, as if it were going to bucking: or,—it is whiting-time,—send him by your two men to Datchet-mead. 116

MRS FORD. He's too big to go in there. What shall I do?

FAL. [*Coming forward*] Let me see't, let me see't, O, let me see't!—I'll in, I'll in.—Follow your friend's counsel.—I'll in. 121

MRS PAGE. What, Sir John Falstaff! Are these your letters, knight?

FAL. I love thee.—Help me away.—Let me creep in here.—I'll never—

[*Gets into the basket; they cover him with foul linen.*

MRS PAGE. Help to cover your master, boy.—Call your men, Mistress Ford.—You dissembling knight!

MRS FORD. What, John! Robert! John!

[*Exit Robin.*

Re-enter Servants

Go take up these clothes here quickly.—Where's the cowl-staff? look, how you drumble!—Carry them to the laundress in Datchet-mead; quickly, come. 131

---

115 *whiting-time*] bleaching-time, spring-time. Cf. *L. L. L.*, V, ii, 893: " And maidens bleach their summer smocks."

124 *I love thee*] Malone and most of his successors add from the early Quartos, *and none but thee*. The words sound like a quotation from some old song. Falstaff had already told Mrs. Ford "I love thee; none but thee," *supra*, line 63.

Enter FORD, PAGE, CAIUS, *and* SIR HUGH EVANS

FORD. Pray you, come near : if I suspect without cause, why then make sport at me ; then let me be your jest ; I deserve it. — How now ! whither bear you this ?

SERV. To the laundress, forsooth.

MRS FORD. Why, what have you to do whither they bear it ? You were best meddle with buck-washing. 137

FORD. Buck ! — I would I could wash myself of the buck ! — Buck, buck, buck ! Ay, buck ; I warrant you, buck ; and of the season too, it shall appear. [*Exeunt Servants with the basket.*] Gentlemen, I have dreamed to-night ; I 'll tell you my dream. Here, here, here be my keys : ascend my chambers ; search, seek, find out : I 'll warrant we 'll unkennel the fox. Let me stop this way first. [*Locking the door.*] So, now uncape.

PAGE. Good Master Ford, be contented : you wrong yourself too much.

FORD. True, Master Page. Up, gentlemen ; you shall see sport anon : follow me, gentlemen. [*Exit.* 149

EVANS. This is fery fantastical humours and jealousies.

CAIUS. By gar, 't is no the fashion of France ; it is not jealous in France.

PAGE. Nay, follow him, gentlemen ; see the issue of his search. [*Exeunt Page, Caius, and Evans.*

---

137 *buck-washing*] See *supra*, l. 2, and note.

145 *uncape*] No other example of this word is found. The meaning is obviously "uncouple" (of hounds in hunting). "Cape" was occasionally used in the sense of "collar." Cf. Madden's *Diary of William Silence,* p. 177, footnote 3.

MRS PAGE. Is there not a double excellency in this?

MRS FORD. I know not which pleases me better, that my husband is deceived, or Sir John.

MRS PAGE. What a taking was he in when your husband asked who was in the basket!

MRS FORD. I am half afraid he will have need of washing; so throwing him into the water will do him a benefit.   161

MRS PAGE. Hang him, dishonest rascal! I would all of the same strain were in the same distress.

MRS FORD. I think my husband hath some special suspicion of Falstaff's being here; for I never saw him so gross in his jealousy till now.

MRS PAGE. I will lay a plot to try that; and we will yet have more tricks with Falstaff: his dissolute disease will scarce obey this medicine.   16

MRS FORD. Shall we send that foolish carrion, Mistress Quickly, to him, and excuse his throwing into the water; and give him another hope, to betray him to another punishment?

MRS PAGE. We will do it: let him be sent for tomorrow, eight o'clock, to have amends.

Re-enter FORD, PAGE, CAIUS, *and* SIR HUGH EVANS

FORD. I cannot find him: may be the knave bragged of that he could not compass.

---

163 *the same strain*] Cf. II, i, 77 and note, *supra.*
170 *carrion*] a term of contempt. Capulet calls Juliet " you greensickness *carrion!*" *Rom. and Jul.,* III, v, 156.

MRS PAGE. [*Aside to Mrs Ford*] Heard you that?

MRS FORD. You use me well, Master Ford, do you?

FORD. Ay, I do so.   180

MRS FORD. Heaven make you better than your thoughts!

FORD. Amen!

MRS PAGE. You do yourself mighty wrong, Master Ford.

FORD. Ay, ay; I must bear it.

EVANS. If there be any pody in the house, and in the chambers, and in the coffers, and in the presses, heaven forgive my sins at the day of judgement!

CAIUS. By gar, nor I too: there is no bodies.

PAGE. Fie, fie, Master Ford! are you not ashamed? What spirit, what devil suggests this imagination? I would not ha' your distemper in this kind for the wealth of Windsor Castle.   193

FORD. 'T is my fault, Master Page: I suffer for it.

EVANS. You suffer for a pad consciencē: your wife is as honest a 'omans as I will desires among five thousand, and five hundred too.

CAIUS. By gar, I see 't is an honest woman.

FORD. Well, I promised you a dinner. — Come, come, walk in the Park: I pray you, pardon me; I will hereafter make known to you why I have done this. — Come, wife; come, Mistress Page. — I pray you, pardon me; pray heartily pardon me.   203

PAGE. Let's go in, gentlemen; but, trust me, we 'll

---

179 *You use me well*] Theobald prefixed the words *Ay, ay; peace*: from the early Quartos.

mock him. I do invite you to-morrow morning to my
house to breakfast : after, we 'll a-birding together ; I
have a fine hawk for the bush. Shall it be so ?

FORD. Any thing.

EVANS. If there is one, I shall make two in the
company.   210

CAIUS. If there be one or two, I shall make-a the turd.

FORD. Pray you, go, Master Page.

EVANS. I pray you now, remembrance to-morrow on
the lousy knave, mine host.

CAIUS. Dat is good ; by gar, with all my heart !

EVANS. A lousy knave, to have his gibes and his
mockeries !   [*Exeunt.*

SCENE IV — A ROOM IN PAGE'S HOUSE

Enter FENTON *and* ANNE PAGE

FENT. I see I cannot get thy father's love ;
Therefore no more turn me to him, sweet Nan.

ANNE. Alas, how then ?

FENT.   Why, thou must be thyself.
He doth object I am too great of birth ;
And that, my state being gall'd with my expense,
I seek to heal it only by his wealth :
Besides these, other bars he lays before me, —
My riots past, my wild societies ;
And tells me 't is a thing impossible
I should love thee but as a property.   10

---

8 *societies*] associates, companions.

ANNE. May be he tells you true.

FENT. No, heaven so speed me in my time to come !
Albeit I will confess thy father's wealth
Was the first motive that I woo'd thee, Anne:
Yet, wooing thee, I found thee of more value
Than stamps in gold or sums in sealed bags ;
And 't is the very riches of thyself
That now I aim at.

ANNE.   Gentle Master Fenton,
Yet seek my father's love ; still seek it, sir :
If opportunity and humblest suit   20
Cannot attain it, why, then, — hark you hither !

                                        [*They converse apart.*

Enter SHALLOW, SLENDER, *and* MISTRESS QUICKLY

SHAL. Break their talk, Mistress Quickly: my kins-
man shall speak for himself.

SLEN. I 'll make a shaft or a bolt on 't : 'slid, 't is but
venturing.

SHAL. Be not dismayed.

SLEN. No, she shall not dismay me: I care not for
that, but that I am afeard.

QUICK. Hark ye ; Master Slender would speak a
word with you.   30

---

16 *stamps in gold*] Cf. *Macb.*, IV, iii, 153, "*a golden stamp*," i. e. a
    coin.
24 *shaft or a bolt*] proverbial expression for "I 'll do it one way or
    another." A shaft was a long, slender arrow ; a bolt, a short,
    thick one.

ANNE. I come to him. [*Aside*] This is my father's choice.

O, what a world of vile ill-favour'd faults
Looks handsome in three hundred pounds a-year!

QUICK. And how does good Master Fenton? Pray you, a word with you.

SHAL. She's coming; to her, coz. O boy, thou hadst a father!

SLEN. I had a father, Mistress Anne; my uncle can tell you good jests of him. Pray you, uncle, tell Mistress Anne the jest, how my father stole two geese out 40 of a pen, good uncle.

SHAL. Mistress Anne, my cousin loves you.

SLEN. Ay, that I do; as well as I love any woman in Gloucestershire.

SHAL. He will maintain you like a gentlewoman.

SLEN. Ay, that I will, come cut and long-tail, under the degree of a squire.

SHAL. He will make you a hundred and fifty pounds ointure.

ANNE. Good Master Shallow, let him woo for himself. 50

SHAL. Marry, I thank you for it; 1 thank you for that good comfort. She calls you, coz: I'll leave you.

ANNE. Now, Master Slender,—

32-33 *O, what . . . a year!*] Cf. *Two Gent.*, III, i, 355, 356, where a woman's *faults* are said to be made *gracious* by a wealthy dowry.
46 *come cut and long-tail*] whatever come, alluding to dogs with short and long tails; equivalent to "bob-tag and rag-tail."

SLEN. Now, good Mistress Anne, —

ANNE. What is your will?

SLEN. My will! od's heartlings, that's a pretty jest
indeed! I ne'er made my will yet, I thank heaven; I
am not such a sickly creature, I give heaven praise.

ANNE. I mean, Master Slender, what would you
with me? 60

SLEN. Truly, for mine own part, I would little or
nothing with you. Your father and my uncle hath
made motions: if it be my luck, so; if not, happy man
be his dole! They can tell you how things go better
that I can: you may ask your father; here he comes.

Enter PAGE *and* MISTRESS PAGE

PAGE. Now, Master Slender: love him, daughter
      Anne. —
Why, how now! what does Master Fenton here?
You wrong me, sir, thus still to haunt my house:
I told you, sir, my daughter is disposed of.

FENT. Nay, Master Page, be not impatient. 70

MRS PAGE. Good Master Fenton, come not to my
      child.

PAGE. She is no match for you.

FENT. Sir, will you hear me?

PAGE.   No, good Master Fenton.

56, 57 *will* . . . *will*] See for the same pun *Merch. of Ven.*, I, ii, 21–22,
  and note.

63 *happy man be his dole*] good fortune go with you. Cf. *T. of Shrew*,
  I, i, 135.

Come, Master Shallow; come, son Slender, in.
Knowing my mind, you wrong me, Master Fenton.

[*Exeunt Page, Shal., and Slen.*

QUICK. Speak to Mistress Page.

FENT. Good Mistress Page, for that I love your
daughter
In such a righteous fashion as I do,
Perforce, against all checks, rebukes and manners,
I must advance the colours of my love, 80
And not retire: let me have your good will.

ANNE. Good mother, do not marry me to yond fool.

MRS PAGE. I mean it not; I seek you a better
husband.

QUICK. That's my master, master doctor.

ANNE. Alas, I had rather be set quick i' the earth,
And bowl'd to death with turnips!

MRS PAGE. Come, trouble not yourself. Good Mas-
ter Fenton,
I will not be your friend nor enemy:
My daughter will I question how she loves you,
And as I find her, so am I affected. 90
Till then farewell, sir: she must needs go in;
Her father will be angry.

FENT. Farewell, gentle mistress: farewell, Nan.

[*Exeunt Mrs Page and Anne.*

---

80 *I must advance the colours*] For the metaphor cf. *L. L. L.*, III, i,
177, 178: "And I to be a corporal of his [Cupid's] field and wear
his colours."

85–86] *Alas, I had rather . . . turnips*] Cf. Ben Jonson, *Bartholomew
Fair*: "Would I had been *set in the ground*, all but the head of
me, . . . and had *my brains bowl'd at.*"

QUICK. This is my doing now: "Nay," said I, "will
you cast away your child on a fool, and a physician?
Look on Master Fenton:" this is my doing.

FENT. I thank thee; and I pray thee, once to-night
Give my sweet Nan this ring: there's for thy pains.   96

QUICK. Now heaven send thee good fortune! [*Exit
Fenton.*] A kind heart he hath: a woman would run
through fire and water for such a kind heart. But yet
I would my master had Mistress Anne; or I would
Master Slender had her; or, in sooth, I would Master
Fenton had her: I will do what I can for them all
three; for so I have promised, and I'll be as good as my
word; but speciously for Master Fenton. Well, I
must of another errand to Sir John Falstaff from my
two mistresses: what a beast am I to slack it!   [*Exit.*

SCENE V—A ROOM IN THE GARTER INN

Enter FALSTAFF and BARDOLPH

FAL. Bardolph, I say, —
BARD. Here, sir.
FAL. Go fetch me a quart of sack; put a toast in 't.
[*Exit Bard.*] Have I lived to be carried in a basket, like
a barrow of butcher's offal, and to be thrown in the

---

95 *a fool, and a physician*] The two words were constantly brought
together colloquially, apparently in vague allusion to the proverbial phrase, "A man of forty is either a fool or his own physician."
Some editors read *or* for *and*.
106 *speciously*] blunder for "especially," as at IV, v, 103, *infra.*

Thames? Well, if I be served such another trick, I'll have my brains ta'en out, and buttered, and give them to a dog for a new-year's gift. The rogues slighted me into the river with as little remorse as they would have drowned a blind bitch's puppies, fifteen i' the litter : and you may know by my size that I have a kind of alacrity 10 in sinking ; if the bottom were as deep as hell, I should down. I had been drowned, but that the shore was shelvy and shallow, — a death that I abhor ; for the water swells a man ; and what a thing should I have been when I had been swelled ! I should have been a mountain of mummy.

Re-enter BARDOLPH *with sack.*

BARD. Here's Mistress Quickly, sir, to speak with you.

FAL. Come, let me pour in some sack to the Thames water ; for my belly's as cold as if I had swallowed snowballs for pills to cool the reins. Call her in. 20

BARD. Come in, woman !

Enter MISTRESS QUICKLY

QUICK. By your leave ; I cry you mercy : give your worship good morrow.

FAL. Take away these chalices. Go brew me a pottle of sack finely.

BARD. With eggs, sir ?

---

9 *blind bitch's puppies*] a colloquial inversion for a "bitch's blind puppies."

FAL. Simple of itself; I 'll no pullet-sperm in my brewage. [*Exit Bardolph.*] How now!

QUICK. Marry, sir, I come to your worship from Mistress Ford. 30

FAL. Mistress Ford! I have had ford enough; I was thrown into the ford; I have my belly full of ford.

QUICK. Alas the day! good heart, that was not her fault: she does so take on with her men; they mistook their erection.

FAL. So did I mine, to build upon a foolish woman's promise.

QUICK. Well, she laments, sir, for it, that it would yearn your heart to see it. Her husband goes this morning a-birding; she desires you once more to come 40 to her between eight and nine: I must carry her word quickly: she 'll make you amends, I warrant you.

FAL. Well, I will visit her: tell her so; and bid her think what a man is: let her consider his frailty, and then judge of my merit.

QUICK. I will tell her.

FAL. Do so. Between nine and ten, sayest thou?

QUICK. Eight and nine, sir.

FAL. Well, be gone: I will not miss her.

QUICK. Peace be with you, sir.   [*Exit.* 50

FAL. I marvel I hear not of Master Brook; he sent me word to stay within: I like his money well. — O, here he comes.

---

34 *take on with*] rage at, get in a passion with. Cf. IV, ii, 18, *infra,*
   " He so *takes on* yonder *with* my husband."
35 *erection*] blunder for " direction."

[88]

Enter FORD

FORD. Bless you, sir!

FAL. Now, Master Brook, — you come to know what hath passed between me and Ford's wife?

FORD. That, indeed, Sir John, is my business.

FAL. Master Brook, I will not lie to you: I was at her house the hour she appointed me.

FORD. And sped you, sir?   6(

FAL. Very ill-favouredly, Master Brook.

FORD. How so, sir? Did she change her determination?

FAL. No, Master Brook; but the peaking Cornuto her husband, Master Brook, dwelling in a continual 'larum of jealousy, comes me in the instant of our encounter, after we had embraced, kissed, protested, and, as it were, spoke the prologue of our comedy; and at his heels a rabble of his companions, thither provoked and instigated by his distemper, and, forsooth, to search his house for his wife's love.   7(

FORD. What, while you were there?

FAL. While I was there.

FORD. And did he search for you, and could not find you?

FAL. You shall hear. As good luck would have it, comes in one Mistress Page; gives intelligence of Ford's approach; and, in her invention and Ford's wife's distraction, they conveyed me into a buck-basket.

FORD. A buck-basket!

FAL. By the Lord, a buck-basket! — rammed me in

with foul shirts and smocks, socks, foul stockings, greasy
napkins; that, Master Brook, there was the rankest compound of villanous smell that ever offended nostril.

FORD. And how long lay you there?

FAL. Nay, you shall hear, Master Brook, what I have
suffered to bring this woman to evil for your good.
Being thus crammed in the basket, a couple of Ford's
knaves, his hinds, were called forth by their mistress to
carry me in the name of foul clothes to Datchet-lane:
they took me on their shoulders; met the jealous knave
their master in the door, who asked them once or twice 90
what they had in their basket: I quaked for fear, lest
the lunatic knave would have searched it; but fate,
ordaining he should be a cuckold, held his hand.
Well: on went he for a search, and away went I for
foul clothes. But mark the sequel, Master Brook: I
suffered the pangs of three several deaths; first, an intolerable fright, to be detected with a jealous rotten bell-
wether; next, to be compassed, like a good bilbo, in
the circumference of a peck, hilt to point, heel to head, 99
and then, to be stopped in, like a strong distillation,
with stinking clothes that fretted in their own grease:
think of that, — a man of my kidney, — think of that,
— that am as subject to heat as butter; a man of continual dissolution and 'thaw: it was a miracle to 'scape
suffocation. And in the height of this bath, when I

---

97 *detected with*] detected by. The usage is common. Cf. *Jul. Cæs.*,
  III, ii, 197: "Here is himself, marr'd, as you see, *with* traitors."
98 *bilbo*] the blade of a bilbo, *i. e.* a Spanish sword from Bilbao, which
  was extremely flexible and elastic. Cf. I, i, 146, *supra*.

was more than half stewed in grease, like a Dutch dish, to be thrown into the Thames, and cooled, glowing hot, in that surge, like a horse-shoe; think of that, — hissing hot, — think of that, Master Brook.

FORD. In good sadness, sir, I am sorry that for my sake you have suffered all this. My suit, then, is desperate; you 'll undertake her no more? 111

FAL. Master Brook, I will be thrown into Etna, as I have been into Thames, ere I will leave her thus. Her husband is this morning gone a-birding: I have received from her another embassy of meeting; 'twixt eight and nine is the hour, Master Brook.

FORD. 'T is past eight already, sir.

FAL. Is it? I will then address me to my appointment. Come to me at your convenient leisure, and you shall know how I speed; and the conclusion shall be crowned with your enjoying her. Adieu. You shall have her, Master Brook; Master Brook, you shall cuckold Ford. [Exit. 122

FORD. Hum! ha! is this a vision? is this a dream? do I sleep? Master Ford, awake! awake, Master Ford! there's a hole made in your best coat, Master Ford. This 't is to be married! this 't is to have linen and buck-baskets! Well, I will proclaim myself what I am: I will now take the lecher; he is at my house; he cannot 'scape me; 'tis impossible he should; he cannot creep into a halfpenny purse, nor into a pepper-box: but, lest

109 *In good sadness*] In sober earnest. Cf. IV, ii, 93, *infra*, and note on *T. of Shrew*, V, ii, 63.

129 *halfpenny purse*] The halfpenny, which was of silver, was a very

the devil that guides him should aid him, I will search
impossible places. Though what I am I cannot avoid,
yet to be what I would not shall not make me tame:
if I have horns to make one mad, let the proverb go
with me, — I 'll be horn-mad. [*Exit.* 134

small coin. Cf. Bacon's *Essays*, 1597, Dedication: "The new
halfpence which, though the silver were good, yet the pieces were
small."

ACT FOURTH — SCENE I
A STREET

Enter MISTRESS PAGE, MISTRESS QUICKLY, *and* WILLIAM

MRS PAGE

S HE AT MASTER FORD'S already, think'st thou?

QUICK. Sure he is by this, or will be presently: but, truly, he is very courageous mad about his throwing into the water. Mistress Ford desires you to come suddenly.

MRS PAGE. I'll be with her by and by; I'll but bring my young man here to school. Look, where his master comes; 'tis a playing-day, I see.

Enter SIR HUGH EVANS

How now, Sir Hugh! no school to-day?

EVANS. No; Master Slender is let the boys leave to 10 play.

QUICK. Blessing of his heart!

MRS PAGE. Sir Hugh, my husband says my son profits nothing in the world at his book. I pray you, ask him some questions in his accidence.

EVANS. Come hither, William; hold up your head; come.

MRS PAGE. Come on, sirrah; hold up your head; answer your master, be not afraid.

EVANS. William, how many numbers is in nouns?

WILL. Two.   90

QUICK. Truly, I thought there had been one number more, because they say, "Od's nouns."

EVANS. Peace your tattlings! What is "fair," William?

WILL. Pulcher.

QUICK. Polecats! there are fairer things than pole-cats, sure.

EVANS. You are a very simplicity 'oman: I pray you, peace.—What is "lapis," William?

WILL. A stone.

EVANS. And what is "a stone," William?   SC

WILL. A pebble.

EVANS. No, it is "lapis": I pray you, remember in your prain.

WILL. Lapis.

EVANS. That is a good William. What is he, William, that does lend articles?

Act IV, Sc. I] This scene is omitted from the two earliest Quartos. It was first printed in the First Folio.

4 *courageous*] apparently a blunder for "outrageous."

[89]

WILL. Articles are borrowed of the pronoun, and be thus declined, Singulariter, nominativo, hic, hæc, hoc.

EVANS. Nominativo, hig, hag, hog; pray you, mark: genitivo, hujus.   Well, what is your accusative case?   40

WILL. Accusativo, hinc.

EVANS. I pray you, have your remembrance, child; accusativo, hung, hang, hog.

QUICK. "Hang-hog" is Latin for bacon, I warrant you.

EVANS. Leave your prabbles, 'oman.—What is the focative case, William?

WILL. O,—vocativo, O.

EVANS. Remember, William; focative is caret.

QUICK. And that's a good root.

EVANS. 'Oman, forbear.   50

MRS PAGE.   Peace!

EVANS. What is your genitive case plural, William?

WILL. Genitive case!

EVANS. Ay.

WILL. Genitive,—horum, harum, horum.

QUICK. Vengeance of Jenny's case! fie on her! never name her, child, if she be a whore.

EVANS. For shame, 'oman.

QUICK. You do ill to teach the child such words:— he teaches him to hick and to hack, which they'll do 60 fast enough of themselves, and to call "horum":—fie upon you!

---

45 *prabbles*] chatter; cf. "pribbles and prabbles," *supra*, I, i, 50, and *infra*, V, v, 153.

60 *hick and to hack*] apparently used in a somewhat ribald significance. See note on II, i, 45, *supra*: "These knights will *hack*."

EVANS. 'Oman, art thou lunatics? hast thou no understandings for thy cases, and the numbers of the genders? Thou art as foolish Christian creatures as I would desires.

MRS PAGE. Prithee, hold thy peace.

EVANS. Show me now, William, some declensions of your pronouns.

WILL. Forsooth, I have forgot.

EVANS. It is qui, quæ, quod: if you forget your 70 "quies," your "quæs," and your "quods," you must be preeches. Go your ways, and play; go.

MRS PAGE. He is a better scholar than I thought he was.

EVANS. He is a good sprag memory. Farewell, Mistress Page.

MRS PAGE. Adieu, good Sir Hugh. [*Exit Sir Hugh.* Get you home, boy. Come, we stay too long. [*Exeunt.*

SCENE II — A ROOM IN FORD'S HOUSE

Enter FALSTAFF and MISTRESS FORD

FAL. Mistress Ford, your sorrow hath eaten up my sufferance. I see you are obsequious in your love, and

---

71 *preeches*] breeches: breeched, *i. e.* flogged.

1-2 *your sorrow . . . love*] your grief has blotted out the memory of my sufferings. I see your devotion (to me) is seriously meant (of the seriousness attaching to funereal rites or obsequies). Cf. *Hamlet*, I, ii, 92, "*obsequious* sorrow."

[91]

I profess requital to a hair's breadth; not only, Mistress
Ford, in the simple office of love, but in all the accou-
trement, complement, and ceremony of it. But are
you sure of your husband now?

MRS FORD. He's a-birding, sweet Sir John.

MRS PAGE. [*Within*] What, ho, gossip Ford! what,
ho!

MRS FORD. Step into the chamber, Sir John.

[*Exit Falstaff.*

Enter MISTRESS PAGE

MRS PAGE. How now, sweetheart! who's at home 10
besides yourself?

MRS FORD. Why, none but mine own people.

MRS PAGE. Indeed!

MRS FORD. No, certainly. [*Aside to her*] Speak louder.

MRS PAGE. Truly, I am so glad you have nobody here.

MRS FORD. Why?

MRS PAGE. Why, woman, your husband is in his old
lunes again: he so takes on yonder with my husband;
so rails against all married mankind; so curses all Eve's
daughters, of what complexion soever; and so buffets 20
himself on the forehead, crying, "Peer out, peer out!"
that any madness I ever yet beheld seemed but tame-
ness, civility, and patience, to this his distemper he is in
now: I am glad the fat knight is not here.

18 *lunes . . . husband*] "Lunes" means "fits of lunacy."

takes on . . . with] gets in a passion with, as at III, v, 34, *supra*,
"she does so *take on with* her men."

21 *Peer out, peer out !*] Horns, make your appearance, come forth !

[92]

MRS FORD. Why, does he talk of him?

MRS PAGE. Of none but him; and swears he was carried out, the last time he searched for him, in a basket; protests to my husband he is now here; and hath drawn him and the rest of their company from their sport, to make another experiment of his suspicion: but I am glad the knight is not here; now he shall see 30 his own foolery.

MRS FORD. How near is he, Mistress Page?

MRS PAGE. Hard by, at street end; he will be here anon.

MRS FORD. I am undone!—the knight is here.

MRS PAGE. Why, then, you are utterly shamed, and he's but a dead man. What a woman are you!— Away with him, away with him! better shame than murder.

MRS FORD. Which way should he go? how should I bestow him? Shall I put him into the basket again?

Re-enter FALSTAFF.

FAL. No, I'll come no more i' the basket. May I 40 not go out ere he come?

MRS PAGE. Alas, three of Master Ford's brothers watch the door with pistols, that none shall issue out; otherwise you might slip away ere he came. But what make you here?

FAL. What shall I do?—I'll creep up into the chimney.

MRS FORD. There they always use to discharge their birding-pieces. Creep into the kiln-hole.

[93]

FAL. Where is it?

MRS FORD. He will seek there, on my word. Neither 50 press, coffer, chest, trunk, well, vault, but he hath an abstract for the remembrance of such places, and goes to them by his note : there is no hiding you in the house.

FAL. I 'll go out, then.

MRS PAGE. If you go out in your own semblance, you die, Sir John. Unless you go out disguised,—

MRS FORD. How might we disguise him?

MRS PAGE. Alas the day, I know not! There is no woman's gown big enough for him ; otherwise he might put on a hat, a muffler, and a kerchief, and so escape. 60

FAL. Good hearts, devise something : any extremity rather than a mischief.

MRS FORD. My maid's aunt, the fat woman of Brentford, has a gown above.

MRS PAGE. On my word, it will serve him ; she's as big as he is : and there's her thrummed hat, and her muffler too. Run up, Sir John.

MRS FORD. Go, go, sweet Sir John : Mistress Page and I will look some linen for your head.

MRS PAGE. Quick, quick! we 'll come dress you 70 straight : put on the gown the while.   [Exit Falstaff.

MRS FORD. I would my husband would meet him in this shape : he cannot abide the old woman of Brentford ; he swears she's a witch ; forbade her my house, and hath threatened to beat her.

---

52 *abstract*] short list or inventory.
66 *thrummed hat*] hat made of coarse yarn.

MRS PAGE. Heaven guide him to thy husband's cudgel, and the devil guide his cudgel afterwards !

MRS FORD. But is my husband coming ?

MRS PAGE. Ay, in good sadness, is he ; and talks of
the basket too, howsoever he hath had intelligence.   80

MRS FORD. We 'll try that ; for I 'll appoint my men
to carry the basket again, to meet him at the door with
it, as they did last time.

MRS PAGE. Nay, but he 'll be here presently : let 's go
dress him like the witch of Brentford.

MRS FORD. I 'll first direct my men what they shall
do with the basket. Go up ; I 'll bring linen for him
straight.   [*Exit.*

MRS PAGE. Hang him, dishonest varlet ! we cannot
misuse him enough.

We 'll leave a proof, by that which we will do,   90
Wives may be merry, and yet honest too :
We do not act that often jest and laugh ;
'Tis old, but true, — Still swine eats all the draff. [*Exit.*

Re-enter MISTRESS FORD *with two* Servants

MRS FORD. Go, sirs, take the basket again on your
shoulders : your master is hard at door ; if he bid you
set it down, obey him : quickly, dispatch.   [*Exit.*

FIRST SERV. Come, come, take it up.

SEC. SERV. Pray heaven it be not full of knight again.

FIRST SERV. I hope not ; I had as lief bear so much 99
lead.

·79 *in good sadness*] in sober earnest. Cf. III, v, 109, *supra,* and note on
T. *of Shrew,* V, ii, 63.

Enter FORD, PAGE, SHALLOW, CAIUS, *and* SIR HUGH EVANS

FORD. Ay, but if it prove true, Master Page, have
you any way then to unfool me again ? Set down the
basket, villain ! Somebody call my wife. Youth in a
basket ! — O you pandarly rascals ! there's a knot, a
ging, a pack, a conspiracy against me: now shall the
devil be shamed. — What, wife, I say ! — Come, come
forth ! Behold what honest clothes you send forth to
bleaching !

PAGE. Why, this passes, Master Ford ; you are not
to go loose any longer ; you must be pinioned.

EVANS. Why, this is lunatics ! this is mad as a mad
dog ! 110

SHAL. Indeed, Master Ford, this is not well, indeed.

FORD. So say I too, sir.

Re-enter MISTRESS FORD

Come hither, Mistress Ford ; Mistress Ford, the honest
woman, the modest wife, the virtuous creature, that
hath the jealous fool to her husband ! I suspect without cause, mistress, do I ?

MRS FORD. Heaven be my witness you do, if you
suspect me in any dishonesty.

FORD. Well said, brazen-face ! hold it out. Come
forth, sirrah ! [*Pulling clothes out of the basket.* 120

PAGE. This passes !

---

103 *a knot, a ging, a pack*] an assembly, a gang, a crowd. " Knot " is
 similarly used, III, ii, 43, *supra,* " a good *knot.*"
119 *hold it out*] keep it up.

MRS FORD. Are you not ashamed? let the clothes alone.

FORD. I shall find you anon.

EVANS. 'T is unreasonable! Will you take up your wife's clothes? Come away.

FORD. Empty the basket, I say!

MRS FORD. Why, man, why?

FORD. Master Page, as I am a man, there was one conveyed out of my house yesterday in this basket: why may not he be there again? In my house I am sure he is: my intelligence is true; my jealousy is reasonable. Pluck me out all the linen. 129

MRS FORD. If you find a man there, he shall die a flea's death.

PAGE. Here's no man.

SHAL. By my fidelity, this is not well, Master Ford; this wrongs you.

EVANS. Master Ford, you must pray, and not follow the imaginations of your own heart: this is jealousies.

FORD. Well, he's not here I seek for. 140

PAGE. No, nor nowhere else but in your brain.

FORD. Help to search my house this one time. If I find not what I seek, show no colour for my extremity; let me for ever be your table-sport; let them say of me, "As jealous as Ford, that searched a hollow walnut for his wife's leman." Satisfy me once more; once more. search with me.

---

143 *show no colour ... extremity*] admit no reasonable pretext for my extreme courses.

MRS FORD. What, ho, Mistress Page! come you and
the old woman down; my husband will come into the
chamber.

FORD. Old woman! what old woman 's that?

MRS FORD. Why, it is my maid's aunt of Brentford. 150

FORD. A witch, a quean, an old cozening quean!
Have I not forbid her my house? She comes of errands,
does she? We are simple men; we do not know what 's
brought to pass under the profession of fortune-telling.
She works by charms, by spells, by the figure, and such
daubery as this is, beyond our element: we know nothing. Come down, you witch, you hag, you; come down,
I say!

MRS FORD. Nay, good, sweet husband!—Good
gentlemen, let him not strike the old woman.

Re-enter FALSTAFF *in woman's clothes, and* MISTRESS PAGE

MRS PAGE. Come, Mother Prat: come, give me your
hand.   161

FORD. I 'll prat her. [*Beating him*] Out of my door,
you witch, you hag, you baggage, you polecat, you
ronyon! out, out! I 'll conjure you, I 'll fortune-tell
you.   [*Exit Falstaff.*

155 *by the figure*] by casting the figure, by calculating the horo-
scope.

156 *daubery*] cheating. The verb "daub" is similarly used.

163 *hag*] This is the reading of the Third and later Folios. The First
and Second Folios read *rag*. But *hag* has already been used at
line 157. "Rag" was, however, occasionally employed as a term
of contempt.

[98]

MRS PAGE. Are you not ashamed? I think you have killed the poor woman.

MRS FORD. Nay, he will do it. 'T is a goodly credit for you.

FORD. Hang her, witch!

EVANS. By yea and no, I think the 'oman is a witch indeed: I like not when a 'oman has a great peard; I spy a great peard under his muffler.   172

FORD. Will you follow, gentlemen? I beseech you, follow; see but the issue of my jealousy: if I cry out thus upon no trial, never trust me when I open again.

PAGE. Let's obey his humour a little further: come, gentlemen.   [*Exeunt Ford, Page, Shal., Caius, and Evans.*

MRS PAGE. Trust me, he beat him most pitifully.

MRS FORD. Nay, by the mass, that he did not; he beat him most unpitifully methought.   180

MRS PAGE. I'll have the cudgel hallowed and hung o'er the altar; it hath done meritorious service.

MRS FORD. What think you? may we, with the warrant of womanhood and the witness of a good conscience, pursue him with any further revenge?

MRS PAGE. The spirit of wantonness is, sure, scared out of him: if the devil have him not in fee-simple, with fine and recovery, he will never, I think, in the way of waste, attempt us again.

174–175 *cry out . . . again*] The expression is drawn from hunting, in
    which the hounds cry out when they find the scent. "Open"
    means "open mouth," "give tongue."
188 *fine and recovery*] See note on *Com. of Errors*, II, ii, 72: "May he

MRS FORD. Shall we tell our husbands how we have
served him?   191

MRS PAGE. Yes, by all means; if it be but to scrape
the figures out of your husband's brains. If they can
find in their hearts the poor unvirtuous fat knight shall
be any further afflicted, we two will still be the ministers.

MRS FORD. I 'll warrant they 'll have him publicly
shamed: and methinks there would be no period to the
jest, should he not be publicly shamed.

MRS PAGE. Come, to the forge with it, then; shape
it: I would not have things cool.   [*Exeunt.* 200

SCENE III — A ROOM IN THE GARTER INN

Enter HOST *and* BARDOLPH

BARD. Sir, the Germans desire to have three of your
horses: the duke himself will be to-morrow at court, and
they are going to meet him.

HOST. What duke should that be comes so secretly?
I hear not of him in the court. Let me speak with the
gentlemen: they speak English?

BARD. Ay, sir; I 'll call them to you.

HOST. They shall have my horses; but I 'll make
them pay; I 'll sauce them: they have had my house a

---

not do it by *fine and recovery ?* " The legal terms imply the fullest
possible right of possession.
193 *figures*] imaginary forms, ideas. Cf. *Jul. Cæs.*, II, i, 231 : " Thou
hast no *figures* [i. e. vain fancies], nor no fantasies, Which busy
care draws in the brains of men."

week at command ; I have turned away my other guests : 10
they must come off; I 'll sauce them. Come. [*Exeunt.*

SCENE IV — A ROOM IN FORD'S HOUSE

Enter PAGE, FORD, MISTRESS PAGE, MISTRESS FORD, *and*
SIR HUGH EVANS

EVANS. 'T is one of the best discretions of a 'oman as
ever I did look upon.

PAGE. And did he send you both these letters at an
instant ?

MRS PAGE. Within a quarter of an hour.

FORD. Pardon me, wife. Henceforth do what thou
   wilt ;
I rather will suspect the sun with cold
Than thee with wantonness : now doth thy honour
   stand,
In him that was of late an heretic,
As firm as faith.

PAGE.   'T is well, 't is well ; no more :   10
Be not as extreme in submission
As in offence.
But let our plot go forward : let our wives
Yet once again, to make us public sport,
Appoint a meeting with this old fat fellow,
Where we may take him, and disgrace him for it.

FORD. There is no better way than that they spoke of.

PAGE. How ? to send him word they 'll meet him in
the Park at midnight ? Fie, fie ! he 'll never come.

EVANS. You say he has been thrown in the rivers, and 20
has been grievously peaten, as an old 'oman: methinks
there should be terrors in him that he should not come;
methinks his flesh is punished, he shall have no desires.

PAGE. So think I too.

MRS FORD. Devise but how you 'll use him when he
       comes,
And let us two devise to bring him thither.

MRS PAGE. There is an old tale goes that Herne the
       hunter,
Sometime a keeper here in Windsor forest,
Doth all the winter-time, at still midnight,
Walk round about an oak, with great ragg'd horns;   30
And there he blasts the tree, and takes the cattle,
And makes milch-kine yield blood, and shakes a chain
In a most hideous and dreadful manner:
You have heard of such a spirit; and well you know
The superstitious idle-headed eld
Received, and did deliver to our age,
This tale of Herne the hunter for a truth.

PAGE. Why, yet there want not many that do fear
In deep of night to walk by this Herne's oak:
But what of this?

MRS FORD. Marry, this is our device;   40
That Falstaff at that oak shall meet with us.

---

31 *takes the cattle*] strikes the cattle with disease. Cf. *Lear*, II, iv, 161–
  162: "Strike her young bones, You *taking* airs, with lameness."
40–41 *Marry . . . us*] This speech is given far more explicitly in
  the First and early Quartos, and thence most editors derive

PAGE. Well, let it not be doubted but he'll come:
And in this shape when you have brought him thither,
What shall be done with him? what is your plot?

MRS PAGE. That likewise have we thought upon, and
        thus:
Nan Page my daughter and my little son
And three or four more of their growth we'll dress
Like urchins, ouphes and fairies, green and white,
With rounds of waxen tapers on their heads,
And rattles in their hands: upon a sudden,   50
As Falstaff, she, and I, are newly met,
Let them from forth a sawpit rush at once
With some diffused song: upon their sight,
We two in great amazedness will fly:
Then let them all encircle him about,
And, fairy-like, to pinch the unclean knight;
And ask him why, that hour of fairy revel,
In their so sacred paths he dares to tread
In shape profane.

MRS FORD.   And till he tell the truth,
Let the supposed fairies pinch him sound,   60
And burn him with their tapers.

---

a third line, *Disguis'd like Herne with huge horns on his head.*
Some such insertion seems necessary to explain the next
speech.

56 *to pinch*] This is the Folio reading, for which editors have substituted *to-pinch*, where "to" is regarded as an intensive prefix.
Such a form is found elsewhere. Cf. Philemon Holland's translation of *Pliny's Nat. Hist.*, X, ch. 74: "Shee will all *to-pinch* and
nip both the fox and her cubs."

[103]

MRS PAGE. The truth being known,
We 'll all present ourselves, dis-horn the spirit,
And mock him home to Windsor.

FORD. The children must
Be practised well to this, or they 'll ne'er do 't.

EVANS. I will teach the children their behaviours;
and I will be like a jack-an-apes also, to burn the knight
with my taber.

FORD. That will be excellent. I 'll go buy them
vizards.

MRS PAGE. My Nan shall be the queen of all the
fairies, 70
Finely attired in a robe of white.

PAGE. That silk will I go buy. [*Aside*] And in that
time
Shall Master Slender steal my Nan away,
And marry her at Eton. Go send to Falstaff straight.

FORD. Nay, I 'll to him again in name of Brook:
He 'll tell me all his purpose: sure, he 'll come.

MRS PAGE. Fear not you that. Go get us properties
And tricking for our fairies.

EVANS. Let us about it: it is admirable pleasures and
fery honest knaveries. [*Exeunt Page, Ford, and Evans.* 80

MRS PAGE. Go, Mistress Ford,
Send quickly to Sir John, to know his mind.
[*Exit Mrs Ford.*

I 'll to the doctor: he hath my good will,
And none but he, to marry with Nan Page.
That Slender, though well landed, is an idiot;
And he my husband best of all affects.

[104]

The doctor is well money'd, and his friends
Potent at court: he, none but he, shall have her,
Though twenty thousand worthier come to crave her.

[*Exit.*

SCENE V — A ROOM IN THE GARTER INN

Enter HOST *and* SIMPLE

HOST. What wouldst thou have, boor? what, thick-skin? speak, breathe, discuss; brief, short, quick, snap.

SIM. Marry, sir, I come to speak with Sir John Fal-staff from Master Slender.

HOST. There's his chamber, his house, his castle, his standing-bed, and truckle-bed; 't is painted about with the story of the Prodigal, fresh and new. Go knock and call; he 'll speak like an Anthropophaginian unto thee: knock, I say.

SIM. There's an old woman, a fat woman, gone up 10 into his chamber: I 'll be so bold as stay, sir, till she come down; I come to speak with her, indeed.

HOST. Ha! a fat woman! the knight may be robbed: I 'll call. — Bully knight! bully Sir John! speak from thy lungs military: art thou there? it is thine host, thine Ephesian, calls.

---

8 *Anthropophaginian*] "Anthropophagi" was the accepted term for
    man-eaters or cannibals.   "Anthropophaginian" is mine host's in-
    vention, and is coined on the analogy of "Carthaginian."
16 *Ephesian*] This word has much the same significance in Elizabethan
    slang as "Corinthian," *i. e.*, a good fellow, a man of mettle.

FAL. [*Above*] How now, mine host!

HOST. Here's a Bohemian-Tartar tarries the coming down of thy fat woman.   Let her descend, bully, let her descend; my chambers are honourable: fie! privacy? 20 fie!

Enter FALSTAFF

FAL. There was, mine host, an old fat woman even now with me; but she's gone.

SIM. Pray you, sir, was't not the wise woman of Brentford?

FAL. Ay, marry, was it, muscle-shell: what would you with her?

SIM. My master, sir, Master Slender, sent to her, seeing her go thorough the streets, to know, sir, whether one Nym, sir, that beguiled him of a chain, had the chain or no.

FAL. I spake with the old woman about it.   30

SIM. And what says she, I pray, sir?

FAL. Marry, she says that the very same man that beguiled Master Slender of his chain cozened him of it.

SIM. I would I could have spoken with the woman herself; I had other things to have spoken with her too from him.

FAL. What are they? let us know.

HOST. Ay, come; quick.

18 *Bohemian-Tartar*] a grandiloquent periphrasis for "gipsy."
25 *muscle-shell*] Simple's lips are agape, like the shells of a mussel.

SIM. I may not conceal them, sir.

HOST. Conceal them, or thou diest.   40

SIM. Why, sir, they were nothing but about Mistress Anne Page; to know if it were my master's fortune to have her or no.

FAL. 'T is, 't is his fortune.

SIM. What, sir?

FAL. To have her, or no. Go; say the woman told me so.

SIM. May I be bold to say so, sir?

FAL. Ay, sir; like who more bold.

SIM. I thank your worship: I shall make my master 50 glad with these tidings.   [Exit.

HOST. Thou art clerkly, thou art clerkly, Sir John. Was there a wise woman with thee?

FAL. Ay, that there was, mine host; one that hath taught me more wit than ever I learned before in my life; and I paid nothing for it neither, but was paid for my learning.

Enter BARDOLPH

BARD. Out, alas, sir! cozenage, mere cozenage!

HOST. Where be my horses? speak well of them, varletto.   60

BARD. Run away with the cozeners: for so soon as I came beyond Eton, they threw me off, from behind one

---

39 *conceal*] blunder for " reveal."

56 *was paid*] was paid out, punished, beaten. The same pun is found in *Cymb.*, V, iv, 161 : " Sorry that you have *paid* too much, and sorry that you are *paid* too much."

of them, in a slough of mire ; and set spurs and away,
like three German devils, three Doctor Faustuses.

HOST. They are gone but to meet the duke, villain :
do not say they be fled ; Germans are honest men.

Enter SIR HUGH EVANS

EVANS. Where is mine host ?

HOST. What is the matter, sir ?

EVANS. Have a care of your entertainments : there is
a friend of mine come to town, tells me there is three 70
cozen-germans that has cozened all the hosts of Readins,
of Maidenhead, of Colebrook, of horses and money.   I
tell you for good will, look you : you are wise, and full
of gibes and vlouting-stocks, and 'tis not convenient
you should be cozened.   Fare you well.   [*Exit.*

64 *Faustuses*] a probable reference to Marlowe's tragedy of *Dr. Faustus.*
    Cf. 1, i, 117, *supra,* " How now, Mephostophilus !"

70-71 *there is three cozen-germans*] There is a plain reference here to a
    contemporary episode of historic importance.   The First Quarto
    reads, *there is three sorts of cosen garmombles.*   "Garmombles"
    seems to be a burlesque rendering of the German name "Mompel-
    gard."   In 1592 Frederick, Duke of Wirtemberg, who was well
    known in England during his stay by his subordinate title of
    Count Mompelgard, was granted official permission to requisition
    post-horses free of charge — a grant which offended innkeepers.
    Count Mompelgard seems to have actually visited inns at Reading,
    Maidenhead, and Colebrook, the places mentioned in the text.
    The mention of "a duke de Jamany" *i. e.* Germany (l. 80) strongly
    supports the identification.   The Duke's journal of his visit to
    England was printed in 1602.

74 *vlouting-stocks*] flouts.   The word with its more regular sense of
    " butts " has already come from Evans' lips, III, i, 108, *supra.*

Enter DOCTOR CAIUS

CAIUS. Vere is mine host de Jarteer?

HOST. Here, master doctor, in perplexity and doubtful dilemma.

CAIUS. I cannot tell vat is dat: but it is tell-a me dat
you make grand preparation for a duke de Jamany: by 80
my trot, dere is no duke dat the court is know to come.
I tell you for good vill: adieu.   [*Exit.*

HOST. Hue and cry, villain, go!— Assist me, knight.
—I am undone!—Fly, run, hue and cry, villain!— I
am undone!   [*Exeunt Host and Bard.*

FAL. I would all the world might be cozened; for I
have been cozened and beaten too. If it should come
to the ear of the court, how I have been transformed,
and how my transformation hath been washed and
cudgelled, they would melt me out of my fat drop by 90
drop, and liquor fishermen's boots with me: I warrant
they would whip me with their fine wits till I were as
crest-fallen as a dried pear. I never prospered since I
forswore myself at primero. Well, if my wind were
but long enough to say my prayers, I would repent.

Enter MISTRESS QUICKLY

Now, whence come you?

QUICK. From the two parties, forsooth.

FAL. The devil take one party, and his dam the
other! and so they shall be both bestowed. I have
suffered more for their sakes, more than the villanous
inconstancy of man's disposition is able to bear.   101

[109]

QUICK. And have not they suffered? Yes, I warrant; speciously one of them; Mistress Ford, good heart, is beaten black and blue, that you cannot see a white spot about her.

FAL. What tell'st thou me of black and blue? I was beaten myself into all the colours of the rainbow; and I was like to be apprehended for the witch of Brentford: but that my admirable dexterity of wit, my counterfeiting the action of an old woman, delivered me, the knave constable had set me i' the stocks, i' the common stocks, for a witch. 112

QUICK. Sir, let me speak with you in your chamber: you shall hear how things go; and, I warrant, to your content. Here is a letter will say somewhat. Good hearts, what ado here is to bring you together! Sure, one of you does not serve heaven well, that you are so crossed.

FAL. Come up into my chamber. [*Exeunt.*

SCENE VI — THE SAME

ANOTHER ROOM IN THE GARTER INN

Enter FENTON *and* HOST

HOST. Master Fenton, talk not to me; my mind is heavy: I will give over all.

FENT. Yet hear me speak. Assist me in my purpose,
And, as I am a gentleman, I 'll give thee
A hundred pound in gold more than your loss.

---

103 *speciously*] blunder for "especially." Cf. III, iv, 106, *supra.*

HOST. I will hear you, Master Fenton; and I will at
the least keep your counsel.

FENT. From time to time I have acquainted you
With the dear love I bear to fair Anne Page;
Who mutually hath answer'd my affection,   10
So far forth as herself might be her chooser,
Even to my wish: I have a letter from her
Of such contents as you will wonder at;
The mirth whereof so larded with my matter,
That neither singly can be manifested,
Without the show of both; fat Falstaff
Hath a great scene: the image of the jest
I 'll show you here at large.   Hark, good mine host.
To-night at Herne's oak, just 'twixt twelve and one,
Must my sweet Nan present the Fairy Queen;   20
The purpose why, is here: in which disguise,
While other jests are something rank on foot,
Her father hath commanded her to slip
Away with Slender, and with him at Eton
Immediately to marry: she hath consented:
Now, sir,
Her mother, even strong against that match,
And firm for Doctor Caius, hath appointed
That he shall likewise shuffle her away,
While other sports are tasking of their minds,   30
And at the deanery, where a priest attends,
Straight marry her: to this her mother's plot

---

16 *fat Falstaff*] The earlier Quartos insert *wherein* before *fat Falstaff*.
The insertion seems necessary to complete the line.

She seemingly obedient likewise hath
Made promise to the doctor.   Now, thus it rests:
Her father means she shall be all in white;
And in that habit, when Slender sees his time
To take her by the hand and bid her go,
She shall go with him: her mother hath intended,
The better to denote her to the doctor, —
For they must all be mask'd and vizarded, —   40
That quaint in green she shall be loose enrobed,
With ribands pendent, flaring 'bout her head;
And when the doctor spies his vantage ripe,
To pinch her by the hand, and, on that token,
The maid hath given consent to go with him.

    Host. Which means she to deceive, father or mother?

    Fent. Both, my good host, to go along with me:
And here it rests, — that you 'll procure the vicar
To stay for me at church 'twixt twelve and one,
And, in the lawful name of marrying,   50
To give our hearts united ceremony.

    Host. Well, husband your device; I 'll to the vicar:
Bring you the maid, you shall not lack a priest.

    Fent. So shall I evermore be bound to thee;
Besides, I 'll make a present recompence.   [*Exeunt.*

---

51 *united ceremony*] uniting ceremony, ceremony of union.

ACT FIFTH — SCENE I

A ROOM IN THE GARTER INN

Enter FALSTAFF *and* MISTRESS QUICKLY

FALSTAFF

RITHEE, NO MORE prattling; go. I'll hold. This is the third time; I hope good luck lies in odd numbers. Away! go. They say there is divinity in odd numbers, either in nativity, chance, or death. Away!

QUICK. I'll provide you a chain; and I'll do what I can to get you a pair of horns.

FAL. Away, I say; time wears: hold up your head, and mince. [*Exit Mrs Quickly.*

Enter FORD

How now, Master Brook! Master Brook, the matter will be known to-night, or never. Be you in the Park 10

8

about midnight, at Herne's oak, and you shall see wonders.

FORD. Went you not to her yesterday, sir, as you told me you had appointed?

FAL. I went to her, Master Brook, as you see, like a poor old man: but I came from her, Master Brook, like a poor old woman. That same knave Ford, her husband, hath the finest mad devil of jealousy in him, Master Brook, that ever governed frenzy. I will tell you:— he beat me grievously, in the shape of a woman; for in the shape of man, Master Brook, I fear not Goliath with 20 a weaver's beam; because I know also life is a shuttle. I am in haste; go along with me: I'll tell you all, Master Brook. Since I plucked geese, played truant, and whipped top, I knew not what 't was to be beaten till lately. Follow me: I'll tell you strange things of this knave Ford, on whom to-night I will be revenged, and I will deliver his wife into your hand. Follow. Strange things in hand, Master Brook! Follow. [Exeunt.

SCENE II — WINDSOR PARK

Enter PAGE, SHALLOW, *and* SLENDER

PAGE. Come, come; we'll couch i' the castle-ditch till we see the light of our fairies. Remember, son Slender, my daughter.

8 *mince*] walk with affected gait, with short steps.
21 *life is a shuttle*] Cf. *Job*, vii, 6: "My days are swifter than a weaver's *shuttle*."
23 *plucked geese*] stripped living geese of their feathers as boys were wont to do.

SLEN. Ay, forsooth; I have spoke with her, and we have a nay-word how to know one another: I come to her in white, and cry, "mum;" she cries "budget;" and by that we know one another.

SHAL. That's good too: but what needs either your "mum" or her "budget"? the white will decipher her well enough. It hath struck ten o'clock. 10

PAGE. The night is dark; light and spirits will become it well. Heaven prosper our sport! No man means evil but the devil, and we shall know him by his horns. Let's away; follow me.   [*Exeunt.*

SCENE III — A STREET LEADING TO THE PARK

Enter MISTRESS PAGE, MISTRESS FORD, *and* DOCTOR CAIUS

MRS PAGE. Master Doctor, my daughter is in green: when you see your time, take her by the hand, away with her to the deanery, and dispatch it quickly. Go before into the Park: we two must go together.

CAIUS. I know vat I have to do. Adieu.

MRS PAGE. Fare you well, sir. [*Exit Caius.*] My husband will not rejoice so much at the abuse of Falstaff as he will chafe at the doctor's marrying my daughter: but 'tis no matter; better a little chiding than a great deal of heart-break. 10

6 "*mum*" . . . "*budget*"] Both were whispered exclamations implying the need of keeping secrets. The words are repeated, line 9, and *infra*, V, v, 186. Cf. Cotgrave's *French-Engl. Dict.*, "To play at *mumbudget*, Demeurer court, ne sonner mot."

MRS FORD. Where is Nan now and her troop of fairies, and the Welsh devil Hugh?

MRS PAGE. They are all couched in a pit hard by Herne's oak, with obscured lights; which, at the very instant of Falstaff's and our meeting, they will at once display to the night.

MRS FORD. That cannot choose but amaze him.

MRS PAGE. If he be not amazed, he will be mocked; if he be amazed, he will every way be mocked.

MRS FORD. We 'll betray him finely.   90

MRS PAGE. Against such lewdsters and their lechery Those that betray them do no treachery.

MRS FORD. The hour draws on. To the oak, to the oak !   [*Exeunt.*

SCENE IV — WINDSOR PARK

Enter SIR HUGH EVANS *disguised, with others as Fairies*

EVANS. Trib, trib, fairies; come; and remember your parts: be pold, I pray you; follow me into the pit; and when I give the watch-'ords, do as I pid you: come, come; trib, trib.   [*Exeunt.*

SCENE V — ANOTHER PART OF THE PARK

Enter FALSTAFF *disguised as Herne*

FAL. The Windsor bell hath struck twelve; the minute draws on. Now, the hot-blooded gods assist me! Remember, Jove, thou wast a bull for thy Europa;

love set on thy horns. O powerful love! that, in some respects, makes a beast a man; in some other, a man a beast. You were also, Jupiter, a swan for the love of Leda. O omnipotent Love! how near the god drew to the complexion of a goose! A fault done first in the form of a beast;—O Jove, a beastly fault! And then another fault in the semblance of a fowl;—think on 't, Jove; a foul fault! When gods have hot backs, what 10 shall poor men do? For me, I am here a Windsor stag; and the fattest, I think, i' the forest. Send me a cool rut-time, Jove, or who can blame me to piss my tallow?—Who comes here? my doe?

Enter MISTRESS FORD *and* MISTRESS PAGE

MRS FORD. Sir John! art thou there, my deer? my male deer?

FAL. My doe with the black scut! Let the sky rain potatoes; let it thunder to the tune of Green Sleeves, hail kissing-comfits, and snow eringoes; let there come a tempest of provocation, I will shelter me here. 20

17–18 *rain potatoes*] Potatoes were in early days reckoned aphrodisiacs, like "eringoes" (the candied root of the sea holly), line 19. Potatoes and eringoes are frequently mentioned together by Elizabethan dramatists in the same significance as in the text. Cf. Beaumont and Fletcher's *Sea Voyage*, III, i, "O for some *eringoes Potatoes* or cantharides." Shakespeare makes only one other reference to potato. Cf. *Troil. and Cress.*, V. ii, 56, "potato-finger," where he again notices its provocative character.

18 *the tune of Green Sleeves*] See II, i, 47, *supra*, and note.

19 *kissing-comfits*] perfumed sugar plums, which made the breath sweet. Shakespeare may have recalled a passage in Holinshed's

Mrs Ford. Mistress Page is come with me, sweetheart.

Fal. Divide me like a bribe buck, each a haunch: I will keep my sides to myself, my shoulders for the fellow of this walk, and my horns I bequeath your husbands. Am I a woodman, ha? Speak I like Herne the hunter? Why, now is Cupid a child of conscience; he makes restitution. As I am a true spirit, welcome!

[*Noise within.*

Mrs Page. Alas, what noise?

Mrs Ford. Heaven forgive our sins L

Fal. What should this be?   30

Mrs Ford. }
Mrs Page. } Away, away!   [*They run off.*

Fal. I think the devil will not have me damned, lest the oil that's in me should set hell on fire; he would never else cross me thus.

Enter Sir Hugh Evans, *disguised as before;* Pistol, *as Hobgoblin;*
     Mistress Quickly, Anne Page, *and others, as Fairies, with*
     tapers.

Quick. Fairies, black, grey, green, and white,
You moonshine revellers, and shades of night,

Chronicle for the year 1583, where in a dramatic performance at
   Court during the scenic presentation of a tempest, " It hailed smal
   confects, rained rose-water, and snew an artificial kind of snow."
22 *bribe buck*] Theobald's emendation of the early reading, *brib'd buck*.
   It probably means a buck of the fine quality bred for giving away
   as bribes or presents.
23-24 *the fellow of this walk*] the forester or gamekeeper.
34 *Enter . . . tapers*] In the early Quartos this stage direction reads

You orphan heirs of fixed destiny,
Attend your office and your quality.
Crier Hobgoblin, make the fairy oyes.

   PIST. Elves, list your names ; silence, you airy toys. 40
Cricket, to Windsor chimneys shalt thou leap :
Where fires thou find'st unraked and hearths unswept,
There pinch the maids as blue as bilberry :
Our radiant queen hates sluts and sluttery.

   FAL. They are fairies ; he that speaks to them shall
        die :
I 'll wink and couch : no man their works must eye.
                    [*Lies down upon his face.*

   EVANS. Where 's Bede ? Go you, and where you find
        a maid
That, ere she sleep, has thrice her prayers said,
Raise up the organs of her fantasy ;
Sleep she as sound as careless infancy : 50
But those as sleep and think not on their sins,
Pinch them, arms, legs, backs, shoulders, sides, and shins.

---

    thus : " Enter Sir Hugh like a Satyre, and boyes drest like
    Fayries, Mistresse Quickly, like the queene of Fayries ; they sing
    a song about him and afterward speake."

37 *orphan heirs . . . destiny*] miraculously conceived inheritors of im-
    mortality. " Orphan heirs " is synonymous with "unfathered
    heirs," in *2 Hen. IV*, IV, iv, 122, an expression applicable to elves
    not begotten of mortal parents, but miraculously created by divine
    or demoniac powers. " Of fixed destiny " is equivalent to " en-
    dowed with immortality," of fixed and unchangeable destiny.

47 *Bede*] This is the name given to the fairy messenger in the Folios.
    The early Quartos read *Pead*, which is probably more in keep-
    ing with Sir Hugh's ordinary dialect.

[119]

Quick. About, about;
Search Windsor Castle, elves, within and out:
Strew good luck, ouphes, on every sacred room;
That it may stand till the perpetual doom,
In state as wholesome as in state 't is fit,
Worthy the owner, and the owner it.
The several chairs of order look you scour
With juice of balm and every precious flower: 60
Each fair instalment, coat, and several crest,
With loyal blazon, evermore be blest!
And nightly, meadow-fairies, look you sing,
Like to the Garter's compass, in a ring:
Th' expressure that it bears, green let it be,
More fertile-fresh than all the field to see;
And *Honi soit qui mal y pense* write
In emerald tufts, flowers purple, blue, and white;
Like sapphire, pearl, and rich embroidery,
Buckled below fair knighthood's bending knee: 70
Fairies use flowers for their charactery.
Away; disperse: but till 't is one o'clock,
Our dance of custom round about the oak
Of Herne the hunter, let us not forget.
    Evans. Pray you, lock hand in hand; yourselves in
                order set;
And twenty glow-worms shall our lanterns be,

---

61 *instalment*] The word which commonly means "installation" seems
    to signify here the "stall" of a knight of the Garter.
71 *charactery*] written cipher; often used in the sense of "short-
    hand."

To guide our measure round about the tree
But, stay ; I smell a man of middle-earth.

FAL. Heavens defend me from that Welsh fairy, lest
he transform me to a piece of cheese !   80

PIST. Vile worm, thou wast o'erlook'd even in thy
birth.

QUICK. With trial-fire touch me his finger-end :
If he be chaste, the flame will back descend,
And turn him to no pain ; but if he start,
It is the flesh of a corrupted heart.

PIST. A trial, come.

EVANS.   Come, will this wood take fire ?
                    [*They burn him with their tapers.*

FAL. Oh, Oh, Oh !

QUICK. Corrupt, corrupt, and tainted in desire !
About him, fairies ; sing a scornful rhyme ;
And, as you trip, still pinch him to your time.   90

SONG

Fie on sinful fantasy !
Fie on lust and luxury !
Lust is but a bloody fire,
Kindled with unchaste desire,

---

78 *middle*] a conventional poetic epithet. In the current astronomical
   system the earth was the *middle* region of the universe, of which
   the upper region was the home of God and the lower region the
   abode of the fairies.

84 *turn him*] put him, a common contemporary usage.

91 *fantasy*] love : see note on *Mids. N. Dr.*, I, i, 32.

92 *luxury*] lasciviousness, incontinence. Cf. *Lear*, IV, vi, 119 : " To 't,
   luxury, pell-mell ; for I lack soldiers."

93 *bloody fire*] fire of blood.

Fed in heart, whose flames aspire,
As thoughts do blow them, higher and higher.
   Pinch him, fairies, mutually;
   Pinch him for his villany;
Pinch him, and burn him, and turn him about,
Till candles and starlight and moonshine be out.   100

During this song they pinch FALSTAFF. DOCTOR CAIUS *comes one
way, and steals away a boy in green;* SLENDER *another way,
and takes off a boy in white; and* FENTON *comes, and steals away
Mrs* ANNE PAGE. *A noise of hunting is heard within. All the
Fairies run away.* FALSTAFF *pulls off his buck's head, and rises.*

Enter PAGE, FORD, MISTRESS PAGE *and* MISTRESS FORD

PAGE. Nay, do not fly; I think we have watch'd you
      now:
Will none but Herne the hunter serve your turn?
MRS PAGE. I pray you, come, hold up the jest no
      higher.
Now, good Sir John, how like you Windsor wives?
See you these, husband? do not these fair yokes
Become the forest better than the town?
FORD. Now, sir, who's a cuckold now? Master
Brook, Falstaff's a knave, a cuckoldly knave; here are

---

100 *During this song . . . rises*] This stage direction is absent from
the First Folio, but it figures in the early Quartos, whence Theobald and succeeding editors have borrowed it.

105 *fair yokes*] This is the reading of the First Folio, which the Second
and later Folios changed to *okes, i. e.* oaks. The reference, of
course, is to the horns, which sometimes take a shape resembling
yokes for cattle. It is less reasonable to identify the horns with the
branches of an oak tree.

his horns, Master Brook : and, Master Brook, he hath en-
joyed nothing of Ford's but his buck-basket, his cudgel,
and twenty pounds of money, which must be paid to
Master Brook ; his horses are arrested for it, Master
Brook.   112

MRS FORD. Sir John, we have had ill luck ; we could
never meet.   I will never take you for my love again ;
but I will always count you my deer.

FAL. I do begin to perceive that I am made an ass.

FORD. Ay, and an ox too : both the proofs are
extant.   117

FAL. And these are not fairies ?   I was three or four
times in the thought they were not fairies : and yet the
guiltiness of my mind, the sudden surprise of my
powers, drove the grossness of the foppery into a received belief, in despite of the teeth of all rhyme and
reason, that they were fairies.   See now how wit may
be made a Jack-a-Lent, when 't is upon ill employment !

EVANS. Sir John Falstaff, serve Got, and leave your
desires, and fairies will not pinse you.

FORD. Well said, fairy Hugh.

EVANS. And leave you your jealousies too, I pray
you.

FORD. I will never mistrust my wife again, till thou
art able to woo her in good English.   130

FAL. Have I laid my brain in the sun and dried it,

---

122 *despite of the teeth of*] An emphatic conjunction of " despite " and
" in the teeth of."
123 *Jack-a-Lent*] See *supra*, III, iii, 22, where the word has already
been cited and explained.

that it wants matter to prevent so gross o'erreaching as this? Am I ridden with a Welsh goat too? shall I have a coxcomb of frize? 'T is time I were choked with a piece of toasted cheese.

EVANS. Seese is not good to give putter; your pelly is all putter.

FAL. "Seese" and "putter"? Have I lived to stand at the taunt of one that makes fritters of English? This is enough to be the decay of lust and late-walking through the realm. 140

MRS PAGE. Why, Sir John, do you think, though we would have thrust virtue out of our hearts by the head and shoulders, and have given ourselves without scruple to hell, that ever the devil could have made you our delight?

FORD. What, a hodge-pudding? a bag of flax?

MRS PAGE. A puffed man?

PAGE. Old, cold, withered, and of intolerable entrails?

FORD. And one that is as slanderous as Satan?

PAGE. And as poor as Job?

FORD. And as wicked as his wife? 150

EVANS. And given to fornications, and to taverns, and sack, and wine, and metheglins, and to drinkings, and swearings, and starings, pribbles and prabbles?

FAL. Well, I am your theme: you have the start of

---

134 *a coxcomb of frize*] A professional fool's cap made of the rough woollen cloth which was a leading Welsh manufacture.

153 *pribbles and prabbles*] See note on I, i, 50, *supra*, and cf. IV, i, 45, *supra*, " leave your *prabbles*."

me; I am dejected; I am not able to answer the Welsh
flannel: ignorance itself is a plummet o'er me: use me
as you will.

FORD. Marry, sir, we 'll bring you to Windsor, to one
Master Brook, that you have cozened of money, to
whom you should have been a pandar: over and above
that you have suffered, I think to repay that money
will be a biting affliction.   162

PAGE. Yet be cheerful, knight: thou shalt eat a posset to-night at my house; where I will desire thee to
laugh at my wife, that now laughs at thee: tell her
Master Slender hath married her daughter.

MRS PAGE. [*Aside.*] Doctors doubt that: if Anne
Page be my daughter, she is, by this, Doctor Caius'
wife.

Enter SLENDER

SLEN. Whoa, ho! ho, father Page!

PAGE. Son, how now! how now, son! have you dispatched?   171

SLEN. Dispatched! I 'll make the best in Gloucestershire know on 't; would I were hanged, la, else!

PAGE. Of what, son?

SLEN. I came yonder at Eton to marry Mistress
Anne Page, and she's a great lubberly boy. If it had

---

156 *ignorance . . . plummet o'er me*] ignorance, helplessness overcomes
    me with its leaden weight. "Plummet" is the weight of lead
    attached to the "plumbline." Cf. Shirley's *Love in Amaze*, IV, 2:
    "What! art melancholy? What hath hung *plummets* on thy
    nimble soul?"

not been i' the church, I would have swinged him, or he should have swinged me. If I did not think it had been Anne Page, would I might never stir! — and 't is a post-master's boy.

PAGE. Upon my life, then, you took the wrong. 180

SLEN. What need you tell me that? I think so, when I took a boy for a girl. If I had been married to him, for all he was in woman's apparel, I would not have had him.

PAGE. Why, this is your own folly. Did not I tell you how you should know my daughter by her garments?

SLEN. I went to her in white, and cried "mum," and she cried "budget," as Anne and I had appointed; and yet it was not Anne, but a postmaster's boy.

MRS PAGE. Good George, be not angry: I knew of your purpose; turned my daughter into green; and, in-deed, she is now with the doctor at the deanery, and there married. 192

Enter CAIUS

CAIUS. Vere is Mistress Page? By gar, I am cozened: I ha' married un garçon, a boy; un paysan, by gar, a boy; it is not Anne Page: by gar, I am cozened.

MRS PAGE. Why, did you take her in green?

CAIUS. Ay, by gar, and 't is a boy: by gar, I 'll raise all Windsor. [*Exit.*

FORD. This is strange. Who hath got the right Anne?

186–187 "*mum*" . . . "*budget*"] See note on V, ii, 6, *supra.*

PAGE. My heart misgives me: — here comes Master
Fenton.   201

Enter FENTON *and* ANNE PAGE

How now, Master Fenton!

ANNE. Pardon, good father! good my mother,
pardon!

PAGE. Now, mistress, how chance you went not with
Master Slender?

MRS PAGE. Why went you not with master doctor,
              maid?

FENT. You do amaze her: hear the truth of it.
You would have married her most shamefully,
Where there was no proportion held in love.
The truth is, she and I, long since contracted,   210
Are now so sure that nothing can dissolve us.
The offence is holy that she hath committed;
And this deceit loses the name of craft,
Of disobedience, or unduteous title;
Since therein she doth evitate and shun
A thousand irreligious cursed hours,
Which forced marriage would have brought upon her.

FORD. Stand not amazed; here is no remedy:
In love the heavens themselves do guide the state;
Money buys lands, and wives are sold by fate.   220

FAL. I am glad, though you have ta'en a special stand
to strike at me, that your arrow hath glanced.

---

221 *stand*] a hiding place in the forest, whence the huntsman aims his
    arrow at the deer. Cf. *L. L. L.*, IV, i, 10.

[127]

_E._ Well, what remedy ? Fenton, heaven give
          thee joy !
What cannot be eschew'd must be embraced.

FAL. When night-dogs run, all sorts of deer are
chased.

MRS PAGE. Well, I will muse no further. Master
          Fenton,
Heaven give you many, many merry days !
Good husband, let us every one go home,
And laugh this sport o'er by a country fire ;
Sir John and all.

FORD.   Let it be so.   Sir John,   230
To Master Brook you yet shall hold your word ;
For he to-night shall lie with Mistress Ford.   [_Exeunt._

CPSIA information can be obtained
at www.ICGtesting.com
Printed in the USA
BVHW052124110221
599826BV00005B/220

9 780469 609631